YOUR RIGHT TO PRIVACY

Minimize Your Digital Footprint

Jim Bronskill and David McKie

Self-Counsel Press
(a division of)
International Self-Counsel Press Ltd.
USA   Canada

Self-Counsel Press acknowledges the financial support of the Government of Canada through the Canada Book Fund (CBF) for our publishing activities.

Printed in Canada.

First edition: 2016

Library and Archives Canada Cataloguing in Publication

Bronskill, Jim, 1964-, author
   Your right to privacy : minimize your digital footprint / Jim Bronskill and David McKie.

ISBN 978-1-77040-263-8 (paperback)

   1. Privacy, Right of. 2. Computer security. 3. Internet—Security measures. 4. Data protection—Security measures.mI. McKie, David, 1959-, author II. Title.

JC596.B76 2016	323.44'83	C2016-901705-2

Dr. Ann Cavoukian, Executive Director of the Privacy and Big Data Institute at Ryerson University and former Information and Privacy Commissioner of Ontario, provided the Foreword and it is used with permission.

Self-Counsel Press
(a division of)
International Self-Counsel Press Ltd.

Bellingham, WA	North Vancouver, BC
USA	Canada

Contents

Notice to Readers

Laws are constantly changing. Every effort is made to keep this publication as current as possible. However, the authors, the publisher, and the vendor of this book make no representations or warranties regarding the outcome or the use to which the information in this book is put and are not assuming any liability for any claims, losses, or damages arising out of the use of this book. The reader should not rely on the authors or the publisher of this book for any professional advice. Please be sure that you have the most recent edition.

Website links often expire or web pages move; at the time of this book's publication the links were current.

Acknowledgments

The idea for this book emerged from the fertile mind of Self-Counsel Press' former Publisher and Editor-in-Chief, Kirk LaPointe. His idea was for Jim and I to write a companion to our first book, *Your Right to Know: How to Use the Law to Get Government Secrets*. His thinking? The right to privacy is the flip side of the right to information. The rationale was as compelling as it was unassailable. This book just had to be written. So I would like to thank Kirk for convincing two initially reluctant and busy working journalists, teachers, and family men to assume this task.

Also deserving of my gratitude is Dr. Ann Cavoukian, whose words grace the book's foreword. She has been a steady, knowledgeable, and passionate voice for privacy rights dating back to her tenure as Ontario's Privacy Commissioner, and now as the Executive Director of Ryerson University's Big Data Institute.

I would also like to thank all the whip-smart experts who patiently guided us through the research and fielded persistent queries about the intricacies of balancing the reasonable expectation of privacy with the need to surrender personal information in order to enjoy the benefits of life in an increasingly connected world.

I would like to, as I always do, thank my wife, Deirdre; son, Jordan; daughters, Hannah Rose and Leila; and son-in-law Scott, whose love fuels the energy and passion needed to take on these projects. Finally, I want to acknowledge the latest addition to our family, my granddaughter,

Nylah Violet. May she grow up in a world that embraces the ideals that fill the pages in this book — our right to privacy.

— DM

❖ ❖ ❖

I would also like to commend Kirk LaPointe for his confidence in us and his belief in the need for such a guide. Special thanks go to David for his willingness to explore new terrain with his customary curiosity and enthusiasm. Thanks also to Tanya Lee Howe for her valuable contributions to organizing and presenting our thoughts.

I came to the project with the advantage of much help over the years from so many people who have informed my reporting on privacy and surveillance issues — to them I express sincere appreciation. Anne-Marie Hayden and her indefatigable team at the federal privacy commissioner's office deserve praise for ably fielding my steady stream of questions. I am also greatly indebted to Colin Bennett, Gus Hosein, and Vincent Gogolek for the insights that greatly enliven the pages that follow.

Finally, I thank Lucianne, Adam, and Rose for their patience, support, and understanding, without which this book could not have been written.

— JB

Foreword

The amount of online data is increasing at an alarming rate. Many of our traditional face-to-face interactions — such as banking, shopping, and social connections — are now taking place online. While more knowledge may lead to undeniable economic and social benefits, the availability of data and specialized analytics that are capable of linking seemingly anonymous information can paint an accurate picture of our private lives. This raises significant concerns about the future of privacy. Preserving privacy may depend on our ability to reclaim control of our online information and personal identities, ensuring continued freedom and liberty via privacy and data protection, in the midst of 21st-century technologies.

We are social animals who seek contact with each other, but we also seek privacy: moments of solitude, intimacy, quiet, reserve, and control — personal control. These interests have coexisted for centuries and must continue to do so, for the human condition requires both. To achieve these competing objectives, organizations must embed easily accessible, privacy-protective controls into their services, or what I call, "Privacy by Design." Equally important, though, must be the willingness of each of us to use them. So while much work is required on the part of organizations to gain our trust that they will be upstanding data custodians, as individuals who also independently contribute to our online identities, we too must shoulder some responsibility for our online privacy.

Your Right to Privacy: Minimize Your Digital Footprint makes a valuable contribution to simplifying the complex online ecosystem into manageable chunks so that each of us is able to understand the implications of our online activities for our privacy. This practical user guide is an encyclopedia of knowledge about privacy and even more, including advice and tips about how we can protect our online identities without needing an advanced degree in science, technology, engineering, or mathematics.

We can, and must, have both — the future of privacy … the future of freedom, may well depend on it. As the saying goes — if you ask for it, it will come. So speak up, get smart, and claim your privacy!

— Dr. Ann Cavoukian,
Executive Director of the Privacy and Big Data
Institute at Ryerson University and former Information and Privacy
Commissioner of Ontario
(ryerson.ca/pbdi/about/people/cavoukian.html)

Introduction

I never said, "I want to be alone." I only said, "I want to be let alone!" There is all the difference.

— Greta Garbo

Digital technology has profoundly changed the way we learn, work, communicate, play, and enjoy culture. It has become such a ubiquitous part of our lives — and brings so many tangible benefits — that we might overlook the not-so-obvious costs.

Perhaps chief among those costs is the surrender of our privacy, threads of personal information from the fabric of our online existence. Sometimes we unknowingly give up the cloak of anonymity through the click of a mouse. But increasingly we are witting participants in handing over personal details as we navigate the online world.

Sharing photos, messages, and our likes and dislikes through social media is fun — not to mention free — and the fact a site such as Facebook harvests our information for commercial purposes in the process just seems part of the bargain. Googling has become a verb, and is now second nature, so we accept the targeted advertising that pops up as a result of our searches.

University of Victoria Political Science Professor Colin Bennett, one of the experts whose opinions we canvassed, put it succinctly: "Our lives are becoming more transparent to multiple organizations."

This book will make you more aware of these transactions, help you better understand them, and show you practical ways to minimize your digital footprint. It is organized around the activities of daily life — at home, at work, in transit, crossing the border and, of course, online.

By the time you read this, there will no doubt be both new ways of interacting with the world that put your privacy at risk and fresh solutions for protecting your personal information. Privacy in the modern age is a fast-moving target, but we hope this guide hits the immediate mark and gives you a sense of where it's all going.

Privacy Principles

The right to privacy has been neatly summarized as the right to be left alone. For our purposes, we will broaden that notion to embrace principles embodied in Canada's federal privacy regime:

- Information should be collected, used, and shared only for specific purposes.

- Data should be stored and disposed of responsibly.

- People should have a right to see information gathered about them.

- Upon being made aware of errors in a personal file, the holder should correct the information.

- People should have the right to complain if personal data is being used for unintended purposes.

In examining an array of issues — from crossing the border to the scourge of identity theft — we will look at how these basic principles apply. Wherever possible, the book will also emphasize what you can do to avoid, address, and remedy potential difficulties each privacy risk might present.

Privacy Through the Ages

In the 11th century, defending England from possible invasion by Scandinavia meant having the funds to maintain a robust army. So in 1086, William the Conqueror undertook an ambitious survey of taxpayers across the land.

One observer noted, "There was no single hide nor a yard of land, nor indeed one ox nor one cow nor one pig which was left out."[1] The epic scale of the endeavor would see it compared to the biblical Judgment Day, or Doomsday, resulting in a sheepskin text composed in black and red ink known as the *Domesday Book*.

It seems governments of various stripes have attempted through history to monitor citizens as a means of enriching the treasury or detecting signs of dissent.

The methods of state control exercised by totalitarian regimes are depressingly familiar: Widespread use of informants, pervasive electronic surveillance, a lack of due process, and arbitrary detention.

In his seminal *1984*, George Orwell describes a rigidly controlled society under the ever-watchful eye of Big Brother — one in which omnipresent telescreens monitor citizens and the Thought Police investigate suspected disloyalty. The novel, published in 1949, seemed to anticipate

---

1   The Domesday Book Online, accessed March 2016. domesdaybook.co.uk/faqs.html

the surveillance states of the Communist Bloc typified by the East German Stasi, which turned neighbor against neighbor in cultivating a vast web of informants.

Though western nations avoided excesses on this scale, the intelligence services of Britain, Canada, and the United States spied on a wide array of citizens who dared question the Cold War political orthodoxy, amassing many thousands of files.

International agreements — including the European Convention on Human Rights and the International Covenant on Civil and Political Rights of the United Nations — began to entrench privacy guarantees. At last count, at least 99 countries have enacted privacy laws.[2]

In Canada, privacy is a quasi-constitutional right enshrined in the *Privacy Act*, governing federal institutions, and the *Personal Information Protection and Electronic Documents Act*, which covers the private sector in concert with similar provincial laws.

A hallmark of the Canadian system is the oversight afforded by the federal privacy commissioner and provincial counterparts, who enforce the laws, serve as ombudsmen for citizens with complaints, and play a watchdog role against invasive practices.

In the United States, the *Privacy Act* governs the collection and use of personal information in the federal government sphere, while the Federal Trade Commission polices the abuse of private data affecting consumers.

Former US spy contractor Edward Snowden's revelations about widespread surveillance of online communication have reverberated in recent years, sparking an international conversation on digital privacy.[3]

In the 21st century, the struggle for privacy is waged not just with governments and law-enforcement agencies but with commercial enterprises that gather, sift, and sell personal data — often without our knowledge but in many cases with our full consent.

The state has a monopoly on a wide range of services and programs that can only be obtained through government, not to mention the ability to restrict or take away our liberty through incarceration, notes Vincent Gogolek, Executive Director of the British Columbia Freedom of Information and Privacy Association.

---

2 "Global Tables of Data Privacy Laws and Bills," (3rd Ed.), Graham Greenleaf, accessed March 2016. papers.ssrn.com/sol3/papers.cfm?abstract_id=2280875
3 "SNOWDEN: Here's Everything We've Learned in One Year of Unprecedented Top-Secret Leaks," Paul Szoldra, accessed March 2016. businessinsider.com/snowden-leaks-timeline-2014-6

This is not to minimize the role of the private sector, which has access to a growing amount of our personal information, Gogolek adds. "But there is increasing convergence between the public and private sectors in terms of information sharing, and also with the delivery of public services through private-sector partners."

University of Victoria Political Scientist Colin Bennett goes further. "I don't think it is possible to tell the difference between the public and private sectors anymore. Governments use the data of the corporate sector for public purposes, and vice versa. In that sense, the Big Brother metaphor is not that useful because the notion of 'the state' has radically changed in the last 30 to 40 years. We need theories of surveillance that go beyond Big Brother and which resonate with the real risks and concerns of the general public."

Against the backdrop of dizzying technological advances, those who wish to minimize their digital footprint find a complex dynamic.

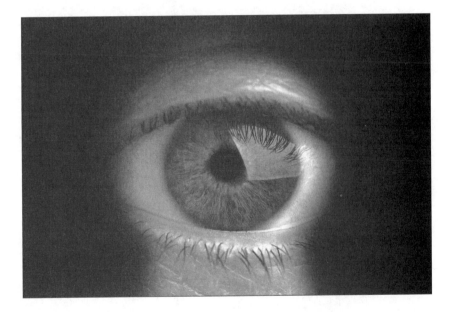

2
Privacy at Home

The sun peeks through the curtains, heralding another day. Before rolling out of bed, you glance at the fitness bracelet attached to your wrist. Padding down the stairs, you notice the living room light is already on and the furnace is waking from its slumber, bringing the temperature up a couple of degrees.

During breakfast, there's a chance to scroll through the headlines on your digital tablet, check the forecast, and browse a few websites for those new shoes you've been meaning to buy.

Before heading out the door, the phone rings. It's someone asking if you want your heating ducts cleaned. Now you're running late, but you're soon out the door and into the car. You remember to slow down at the big intersection where a newly installed camera is tracking speeders. You park your car at the light rail station and reach for your transit pass, swiping it as you board the train for downtown. The journey is about 12 minutes, enough time to do a little online banking on your smartphone.

The security guard makes chitchat as you fill out the sign-in sheet in the lobby of your office building. A quick fumble for your electronic pass card, another swipe and you board the elevator for the seventh floor.

At your desk, you scratch your head before finally remembering your new computer password. Once logged on, you pull a memory key out of your briefcase, insert it into the machine, and retrieve the report you began pulling together last night at home.

During lunch hour, you check a few more websites and find those shoes at a great price from an online wholesaler. You log into your account with the store, confirm your credit card number, and place the order. Then your cell phone rings. It's your spouse reminding you to call the insurance company. Before heading back to the office, there's time to call the company and complete a medical history survey over the phone — a prerequisite for term life insurance.

The day is only a few hours old, but already you have left a potentially revealing trail of personal fingerprints. You probably didn't give it a second thought and, besides, such interactions are just part of everyday life. In the modern era, we have little choice but to part with sensitive data. While that may be true, you can choose to practise good habits that will protect your personal information — and in turn your reputation, credit rating, and livelihood.

We have every right to hope our home would be a private sanctuary from the many people, organizations, and devices collecting information about us. Curtains, blinds, and a good fence are not enough anymore. In this chapter, we explore the nuisance of telemarketers, the techniques political parties use to gather personal information, and the increasingly wired nature of the places we live.

1. Telemarketers

We've all had them: Those annoying calls from telemarketers that always seem to come at the most inconvenient times such as during dinners or family gatherings. The good news is that there are steps you can take to reduce, though not necessarily eliminate, the calls.

In Canada, this is where the Canadian Radio-television and Telecommunications Commission (CRTC) enters the picture. The CRTC is an administrative tribunal that regulates and supervises Canadian broadcasting and telecommunications in the public interest. That means part of its job is to protect you from unwanted calls, faxes, and email.

In the United States, this task belongs to the Federal Trade Commission (FTC), "A bipartisan federal agency with a unique dual mission to protect consumers and promote competition."

In 2006, the Canadian Parliament amended the *Telecommunications Act* to allow the CRTC to establish a national Do Not Call List (DNCL). Telemarketers are required by law to register and pay fees to download updates from a secure website.

The rules apply to all companies that conduct unsolicited telecommunications, whether for themselves or someone else. Not only are telemarketers required to respect the wishes of consumers who have registered their numbers on the list, but they must also maintain their own internal lists.

In the United States the Do-Not-Call Registry has been operating since 2003 and contains similar requirements for consumers and telemarketers. The registry is enforced by the FTC, the Federal Communications Commission, and state officials.

The telemarketer, who can only call within specific hours, must identify on whose behalf the call is being made. There are also rules limiting the use of Automated Dialing-Announcing Devices (ADADs).[1] Telemarketers from the US, and other countries, making calls to Canadian consumers must also follow the same rules.

Though there are many restrictions, certain kinds of telemarketing calls and faxes are exempt from the Canadian DNCL, including those made by or on behalf of:

- Registered charities.

- Newspapers looking for subscriptions.

- Political parties and their candidates.

- Companies with whom you have an existing business relationship.

- Individuals or organizations made solely for the purpose of market research or surveys (they are not considered to be telemarketing calls because they are not selling a product or service, or asking for donations).

- Debt-collection calls.

- Persons or entities to whom you have provided express consent to be called.

If you wish to avoid these telemarketers, you can ask to be put on their Do Not Call Lists, which they are obliged to do within 14 days. It's a good idea to record the date of your request. The organization must keep your number on its do not call list for three years and 14 days.

---

1   Frequently Asked Questions, National Do Not Call List, accessed March 2016. lnnte-dncl.gc.ca/faqs-eng#an_link05

In Canada, you can sign up online (lnnte-dncl.gc.ca) or by calling toll-free (1-866-580-3625). After you sign up, your numbers will be added to the list within 24 hours. Once a number has been registered on the national DNCL, it is permanent. You can also, at any time, have your number removed. In the United States, you can also sign up online (donotcall.gov/register/reg.aspx) or by calling toll free (1-888-382-1222).

Telemarketers then have 31 days to update their own information and make sure they don't call you in their next round of telemarketing. Don't expect all calls to stop immediately. You could still receive calls within the first 31 days of signing up.

Although unsolicited calls can be an annoying fact of life, there are steps you can take to reduce the volume:

- Be careful about providing your number to anyone.

- On forms, always select any privacy check box that indicates you do not wish to be contacted. If there is no privacy option, then be cautious about providing your telephone number to a company.

- You may ask companies you do business with to avoid sharing your telephone number, or any other personal information, with third parties.

1.1 How to complain

If the calls persist once your name is on the list, there are steps you can take which involve getting the caller's phone number and reporting it to the CRTC, along with the date. You may be able to see the telemarketer's number and name from your telephone's call display, or hear the last caller's number by dialing *69. If the telemarketer calls again, ask for a number and name.

If the complaint checks out, the CRTC has many options such as a warning letter, a citation published on the tribunal's website that identifies the alleged violation and specific corrective actions to be taken during an agreed-upon time frame, and a notice of violation for the most serious violations.

If you think the call is part of a fraud scheme, call the federal government's Canadian Anti-Fraud Centre, a central agency that collects information and criminal intelligence on issues such as mass-marketing fraud, Internet fraud, and identification theft complaints.

In the United States, the steps are similar, though the Federal Trade Commission warns individual responses are impossible due to the high volume of complaints. However, this doesn't mean that you're being ignored. On the contrary, the FTC and other law enforcement agencies analyze the complaints for patterns, and then take "aggressive legal action," which includes fines of up to $16,000 per call. So it's always a good idea to complain.

2. Political Parties

Political parties are exempt from privacy legislation, in large part because the political process hinges on parties gaining access to personal information. The challenge is balancing the desire to protect personal privacy with the need to give political parties access to personal data to ensure political participation, the hallmark of any democracy. As we will see throughout this book, privacy advocates, regulatory institutions, businesses, and consumers struggle to get this balance right.

In Canada, the Office of the Chief Electoral Officer, known to most people as Elections Canada, is an independent, nonpartisan agency that reports directly to Parliament. Its responsibilities include conducting federal elections and by-elections and monitoring compliance with the *Canada Elections Act*.

In an age when political parties are devising more sophisticated means of identifying voters to ask them for money and convince them to turn up at the polls to cast a ballot, concerns about privacy should be top of mind. If you receive a request from a political party out of the blue, chances are that the organization obtained your personal information without your knowledge and consent.

At first blush, you might be tempted to blame Elections Canada for disclosing your personal details to a political party. Such was the case of a woman who complained to the Office of the Privacy Commissioner in 2006. The woman, who the commissioner does not name, became concerned when she asked the canvasser how she had obtained her phone number and knew which party she was supporting? The woman was told Elections Canada provided the information.[2]

Now, the *Canada Elections Act* does say that it is acceptable for a registered political party to obtain the electoral list from each polling division. That list will include your name and address. Absent from that

---

2   "Voter Alarmed by Political Party Canvasser's Comments," The Office of the Privacy Commissioner of Canada, accessed March 2016. priv.gc.ca/cf-dc/pa/2006-07/pa_200607_07_e.asp

list, however, is the identity of the political party you supported in the previous election.

Every candidate, member of Parliament, and registered political party is allowed to use the list for communicating with voters. This is why the woman naturally assumed that Elections Canada was the culprit. But was it? It turns out Elections Canada was blameless. The Privacy Commissioner ruled the woman's complaint was not well-founded because Elections Canada had not provided information about her party affiliation. She was also pleased to discover her name could be deleted from the electoral list sent to political parties.

The culprit was never identified, but the woman was right to sound the alarm. At the very least, such complaints put political parties on notice that while democracy depends on engaged voters, their privacy must not be taken for granted.

As we will learn in subsequent chapters, institutions such as political parties and commercial organizations find many ways to make contact with unsuspecting individuals.

In the United States, state and local governments administer federal elections. The specifics of how elections are conducted differ between states, and the US Constitution grants states wide latitude in how they administer elections.

In 2002, the Election Assistance Commission was established by the *Help America Vote Act* to oversee and educate the public about the voting process. The Commission is a valuable clearinghouse for information about voting and registering in your state. To make things easier, many states allow voters to register online.

In Canada, the law defines a political party as an organization whose fundamental purpose is to participate in public affairs by endorsing one or more of its members as candidates and supporting their election.

Section 44 of the Act gives the Chief Electoral Officer the power "to maintain a register of Canadians who are qualified as electors, to be known as the Register of Electors."[3] The law says that the returning officers, or an assistant returning officer, may delete the name of the person from a preliminary list of electors if the person requests it and provides satisfactory proof of identity.

---

3   *Canada Elections Act*, accessed March 2016. documentcloud.org/documents/2691008-Canada-Elections-Act.html#document/p70/a271905

MPs and registered parties have access to the National Register of Electors. It's important to realize that there is a difference between being on the electoral list and in a party's database. The former does not indicate how you vote. The latter does. Parties use a number of methods to glean information about your voting patterns from venues such as social media sites. For instance, friending a political party on Facebook can result in the user's name and photo being listed on the party's social media page.

Parties in the United States and Canada can pass the information they glean to telemarketing agencies, which then place automatic calls, send emails, or post letters to these potential supporters asking for money, or telling them to vote. Since many rules do not apply to political parties, there is little to be done, short of asking the party in question to remove your name from the list.

In addition to being exempt from the Federal Trade Commission rules, CRTC rules, and federal and provincial and public- and private-sector privacy laws, political parties are also exempt from the new anti-spam legislation, and the do-not-call list provisions discussed earlier in section 1.

If you feel your privacy has been breached, it's best to contact the party and ask that your name be removed. It's unlikely that the breach will come from Elections Canada or your state. Chances are, the issue may rest with some aspect of your online activity.

3. A Wired House

As we add devices to our homes ... much more sensitive data will be collected. User interfaces on devices will shrink or disappear, making it more difficult for consumers to know when data is being collected, or to exercise any control. In fact, I expect that the Internet itself will soon "disappear" because connectivity will just be part of how things work, as electricity is today.[4]

— Julie Brill

Our connection to the Internet goes far beyond our computers, mobile phones, and tablets. An increasing number of devices in our immediate surroundings track information about us and upload it to the institution

---

4   "Privacy and Data Security in the Age of Big Data and the Internet of Things," Julie Brill, US Federal Trade Commissioner, accessed March 2016. ftc.gov/system/files/documents/public_ statements/904973/160107wagovprivacysummit.pdf

or organization responsible for delivering a service. For instance, electronic thermostats monitor how much heat we use at certain times of the day, allowing the service provider to gauge consumer demand.

So pervasive is our connectivity to the Internet that a new phrase has been coined to describe the phenomenon: The Internet of Things. It is an environment in which people are connected through their devices that transfer data over a network without requiring human-to-human or computer-to-human interaction.

In its discussion of the Internet of Things, the Office of the Privacy Commissioner of Canada compares the phenomenon to "electricity, or the nervous system for the planet" that has become unseen, pervasive and woven into the "fabric of our society." In general, it concludes that the Internet of Things is a "networking of physical objects connecting through the Internet" that includes elements that are discussed in this book:

- Cheap, ever-present sensors, devices, or "things."

- Connection of the physical objects in our homes, cars, workplaces and bodies with cyberspace.

- Generation of data that is stored in the cloud where it is processed, aggregated, analyzed, and sometimes sold to the highest bidder.

Though it may sound other wordly, the Canadian privacy commissioner points out that the concept is hardly a new one, since devices have been communicating with each other for a number of years. What makes the phenomenon more pervasive are many of the concepts we examine in these pages:

- A growing number of electronic devices are being invented and built to communicate with the Internet through sensors.

- These sensors are increasingly sophisticated.

- The devices communicate a wide range of information, such as your location, biometrics, online shopping preferences and, as we'll see in this section, your viewing habits.

- Internet of Things computing devices are cheaper, more accessible and come in all shapes and sizes. For instance, wearable devices discussed in Chapter 9 like the popular Fitbit which monitors steps taken and calories burned.

- An increasing number of institutions and organizations are using cloud computing and Big Data analytics to store, analyze and share information.[5]

Indeed, the benefits are many — a point that Federal Trade Commissioner Julie Brill stressed at the beginning of the speech she delivered on January 5, 2016:

"Let me be clear at the outset: I believe that big data and the Internet of Things have potentially tremendous benefits. Cities can better maintain their infrastructures by developing sophisticated early warning systems for gas and water leaks. Medical researchers can enroll patients in large-scale research projects and collect streams of useful data that, in the past, would have been a mere trickle coming from surveys and patients' own reports."

However, Brill also warned about the dangers — that is, companies that sell these devices might not spend a lot of time thinking about security until a breach has happened. Samsung and a product it calls a SmartTV is a case in point. The TV's remote control has a feature that, if enabled, allows you to use your voice to perform tasks such as change channels. In its privacy policy, the company had this warning, which was first reported by *The Daily Beast*, on February 2, 2015: "A single sentence buried in a dense 'privacy policy' for Samsung's Internet-connected SmartTV advises users that its nifty voice command feature might capture more than just your request to play the latest episode of *Downton Abbey*.

"Please be aware that if your spoken words include personal or other sensitive information, that information will be among the data captured and transmitted to a third party."[6]

So who was this third-party provider? What information other than your voice command was being picked up? Were errant discussions also being transmitted, and if so, what was being done with the information? If the transmission is not properly encrypted, could a hacker turn your TV into an eavesdropping device?

The day after *The Daily Beast* reported this, the company issued a statement insisting that it uses "industry-standard security safeguards

---

5   The Internet of Things: An introduction to privacy issues with a focus on the retail and home environments, a research paper prepared by the Policy and Research Group of the Office of the Privacy Commissioner of Canada, pp 4-6, https://www.priv.gc.ca/information/research-recherche/2016/iot_201602_e.pdf

6   "Your Samsung SmartTV Is Spying on You, Basically," Shane Harris, *The Daily Beast*, accessed March 2016. thedailybeast.com/articles/2015/02/05/your-samsung-smarttv-is-spying-on-you-basically.html

and practices, including data encryption, to secure consumers' personal information and prevent unauthorized collection or use."[7] That response did little to quell the outrage.

Former Ontario Privacy Commissioner Ann Cavoukian expressed her indignation during an interview with CBC News: "With Samsung, it's like all of a sudden you have to monitor what you should say in your home — the last bastion of privacy, a place that's supposed to be sacrosanct. Are you kidding me?"[8]

In her speech at that International Consumer Electronics Show in Las Vegas, Brill raised concerns about this technology. "To help consumers navigate and benefit from this complex, uncertain, and exciting world, the Internet of Things and big data analytics need to meet consumers' expectations and earn their trust. Appropriate privacy and security protections, as well as broader assurances that consumers are being treated fairly, are key elements of consumer trust."

So what are we to learn from this cautionary tale about the Smart-TV? For Cavoukian, now Executive Director of the Privacy and Big Data Institute at Toronto's Ryerson University, the first step is to read the company's privacy policy very carefully so that you know what information is being collected, how it's being protected, how it's being used, and what happens in case of a security breach.

These policies are dense and make for tough reading, but it's worth the effort. Reputable companies should have robust policies in place. If not, then the negative publicity can force them into action, or at least clarify their position, as we saw in the Samsung case.

If you're still not satisfied, Cavoukian says, the answer is simple: Leave the product on the store shelf.

The general public is coming to appreciate how our possessions can capture and transmit data about our lives, and also how that data can be analyzed to draw conclusions about our "private" behavior, said Colin Bennett, a political scientist at the University of Victoria. "The Internet of Things will gradually complicate the boundary between public and private spaces, and will complicate the question of what is, and is not, personal information."

---

7   "Samsung Smart TVs Do Not Monitor Living Room Conversations," Samsung Newsroom, accessed March 2016. news.samsung.com/global/samsung-smart-tvs-do-not-monitor-living-room-conversations

8   "Samsung SmartTV an 'Absurd' Privacy Intruder, Ann Cavoukian Says," Matt Kwong, CBC News, accessed March 2016. cbc.ca/news/technology/samsung-smarttv-an-absurd-privacy-intruder-ann-cavoukian-says-1.2950982

The Office of the Privacy Commissioner of Canada and its counterparts in the United States and Europe are concerned that policies governing privacy are taking a back seat to the technological developments of the Internet of Things, as more devices explode on to the market.

"How, then, can citizens who may or may not want to use this technology ensure that someone is held accountable for its use? How will they be able to challenge how the information is used, and how will they be able to give any kind of meaningful consent?"[9]

These questions prompted Canada's privacy commissioner, whose office is part of the Global Privacy Enforcement Network, to launch what it calls the Internet of Things 2016 "global privacy sweep."

For its part, Canada's privacy office focused on health devices such as fitness trackers, smart scales, and sleep monitors.[10]

During its sweep, the privacy office looked at "whether users could understand how their personal information is collected, used, disclosed, and safeguarded and whether they could easily contact someone if they had any privacy questions," said Tobi Cohen, a spokeswoman for the commissioner.

Officials had a chance to buy gizmos, try them out, and see if the accompanying privacy communications — the written explanations for users — were sufficient, she said.

"We examined the online information and other privacy communications available to the user related to the company behind the devices; we are contacting manufacturers, retailers and data controllers with specific privacy questions where necessary and we have sought to replicate the consumer experience by assessing privacy communications and information available to the user out of the box through to actual use of the devices."[11]

The office will publicize its results in the fall of 2016.

---

9 Source: The Internet of Things: An introduction to privacy issues with a focus on the retail and home environments, a research paper prepared by the Policy and Research Group of the Office of the Privacy Commissioner of Canada, p. 26, https://www.priv.gc.ca/information/research-recherche/2016/iot_201602_e.pdf
10 Source: "Canada examines health devices during 2016", Office of the Privacy Commissioner of Canada, April 11, 2016, https://www.priv.gc.ca/media/nr-c/2016/nr-c_160411_e.asp
11 Source: Interview with authors, May 4, 2016

3
Employee Privacy Rights

An individual's privacy in the workplace is a balance between the employer's need to collect, use, and — in rare circumstances — disclose personal information and the employee's right to ensure the information is accurate and used correctly.

As is the case with access to information, spelled out in *Your Right to Know: How to Use the Law to Get Government Secrets* (published by Self-Counsel Press), Canadians have a quasi-constitutional guarantee of privacy. Their rights are protected under sections seven and eight of the Canadian Charter of Rights and Freedoms. The sections articulate the "right to life, liberty, and security of the person," and the right to be secure against unreasonable search and seizure, respectively.[1]

No such guarantee exists in the United States where the US Constitution excludes "privacy as a fundamental right or even an important concept." That being said, Americans do enjoy some protections, especially in areas that lawmakers have decided are important to protect such as "financial-account information, health-care-provider data, and any information intentionally taken from children."[2]

When it comes to personal information the US government collects, citizens have rights in broad categories under the *Privacy Act*. Enacted in 1974, the Act guarantees three primary rights: The right to see personal

---

1   *Constitution Act, 1982,* Justice Laws Website, accessed March 2016. http://laws-lois.justice. gc.ca/eng/const/page-15.html
2   *Privacy in the Age of Big Data: Recognizing Threats, Defending Your Rights, and Protecting Your Family,* Theresa M. Payton and Theodore Claypoole, Rowman & Littlefield Publishing Group, 2015, p. 248.

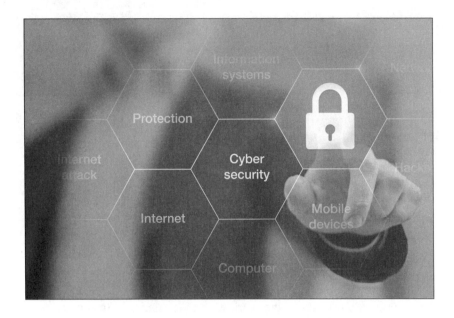

records, subject to the law's exemptions; the right to request that the records be updated for accuracy; and the right against unwarranted invasion of privacy resulting from the "collection, maintenance, use, and disclosure of personal information."[3]

When it comes to the workplace, protection in both countries is limited to the employer's use of the information for purposes that were never intended, such as sharing with a third party. The US Electronic Privacy Information Center puts it this way: "There are no general protections of workplace privacy except where an employer acts tortiously — where the employer violates the employee's reasonable expectation of privacy."[4]

So when it comes to monitoring your activity in the workplace, the employer has the upper hand. That being said, it's important to know the ground rules.

I. What Information Can Your Employer Collect?

Networked computers and other forms of advanced technology allow institutions to collect information in many different ways. Some examples include:

---

3   *Privacy Act*, US Department of State, accessed March 2016. foia.state.gov/Learn/PrivacyAct.aspx
4   "Workplace Privacy," Electronic Privacy Information Center, accessed March 2016. epic.org/privacy/workplace/#introduction

- Background, credit and criminal record checks.

- Résumés, cover letters, and job applications.

- Video surveillance of work premises and off-duty conduct.

- Global positioning systems for couriers, delivery, and transport workers.

- Telephone monitoring.

- Keystroke logging.

- Monitoring of Internet activities.

- "Smart" ID cards that track work attendance, access to the workplace, resources, and drug and dental plans.

- Biometrics (i.e., fingerprint, handprint, voice, and eye scanning to verify employee identity for security purposes).

- Drug and alcohol tests.

- Workplace investigations.[5]

Whether any particular method of collection is permissible depends on the following:

- Employee was aware of the monitoring.

- Consent was obtained.

- Intrusiveness of the collection.

- Appropriate balance between employer and employee interests.

- Facts of the situation.

2. Why Do Employers Need This Information?

Employers are motivated to monitor employees in the workplace due to increased attacks, violence, safety concerns, mishaps, robberies, and associated liabilities and damages. There are also concerns about potential liability resulting from employee computer misuse or misconduct.

---

5   "Workplace Privacy — What Information about Me Can My Employer Gather?" Samuelson-Glushko Canadian Internet Policy and Public Interest Clinic (CIPPIC), accessed March 2016. cippic.ca/FAQ/workplace_privacy/gather

"Racial and sexual harassment claims arising from racist or pornographic Web browsing or emails is not an uncommon occurrence," notes a legal paper about US companies battling liability suits. "Morgan Stanley, the Wall Street brokerage, was sued for (US)$70 million by employees because of racist jokes that were being distributed on its email system and allegedly created a hostile work environment."[6]

A growing number of people are also working from home. Companies use and need systems to monitor employees to identify emergencies, assess productivity, and guard against security breaches, given that there is ample evidence to suggest that most information-technology breaches and crimes are inside jobs.

So companies have legitimate reasons for collecting information, as long as that crucial balance is being maintained.

3. What Steps Can You Take?

If you are on company time, or working in a satellite office or from your home, begin by using common sense. Typically, this means being aware of the company's policies, and making sure that you abide by them. Educate yourself. When it comes to your rights in the workplace, ask questions. For instance:

- Ask to see what information is collected about you, even if the company is not legally required to agree.

- Ask to see the policies for collecting, safeguarding, and eventually destroying the information.

- Ask if this information is shared, and if so why, and under what circumstances.

- Ask about the company's surveillance methods.

- Ask for the policies on web, email, and telephone use. If employees are subject to random or continuous surveillance, they need to be told.

- If your workplace is unionized, ask to see the parts of the collective agreement that govern the terms and conditions of employment. As the Canadian Internet Policy and Public Interest Clinic points out, "Some unions have been successful in advancing their

---

6   "Workplace Monitoring and Surveillance," Christopher McHardy, Tina Giesbrecht, and Peter Brady, accessed March 2016. mccarthy.ca/pubs/Monitoring_and_Surveillance.pdf

members' privacy interests even where such interests are not explicitly protected in legislation or collective agreements."[7]

If there are circumstances in which private information is improperly disclosed within the workplace, or inappropriately shared with a third party, employee privacy interests remain paramount.

---

7   "Workplace Privacy," Samuelson-Glushko Canadian Internet Policy and Public Interest Clinic (CIPPIC), accessed March 2016. cippic.ca/en/FAQ/workplace_privacy

4

Online Security

People have to, at minimum, ask questions about what organizations will do with the personal information they collect from us, and who they will share it with and for what purpose.

— Vincent Gogolek,
Executive Director of the British Columbia
Freedom of Information and Privacy Association

Like bandits prowling on the dirt roads of ancient times, cybercriminals, hackers, and digital spies roam the electronic global village.

Today's world is more interconnected than ever before, but for all its advantages, increased connectivity brings a greater risk of theft, fraud, and abuse, says the US Department of Homeland Security.

"Sophisticated cyber-actors and nation-states exploit vulnerabilities to steal information and money and are developing capabilities to disrupt, destroy, or threaten the delivery of essential services," the department says. "A range of traditional crimes are now being perpetrated through cyberspace."

Organized criminals launder vast sums online. Child pornographers dwelling in the murky depths of the Web make, distribute, and even livestream their vile images. Chinese hackers systematically find their way into foreign computers in search of valuable intelligence.

Although attacks may come from the virtual realm, their consequences are very real, warns the Canadian Security Intelligence Service.

"These hostile players can be foreign intelligence agencies, terrorists, hacktivists, or simply individuals acting alone," the spy service says.

"Moreover, these hostile actors have access to a growing range of cyber-attack tools and techniques. Attackers have employed carefully crafted emails, social networking services, and other vehicles to acquire government, corporate, or personal data."

Breaches of customer information occur with alarming regularity, often involving thousands of files held by large, trusted companies. The lapses have embarrassed corporations and placed the personal details of citizens at risk. For example, Ashley Madison was an online service that promised discretion for married people who wanted to have an affair. However, the veil of secrecy was abruptly lifted when digital vigilantes stole the client data and posted names and credit card details on the Internet.

Government agencies are also victims of online intrusions, and many experience data losses when hard drives or tiny memory keys containing personal details go astray. Such storage devices are convenient because they hold huge amounts of data and are generally small and highly portable, Canadian privacy commissioner Daniel Therrien noted in his latest annual report.[1] That also creates significant privacy and security risks, since the devices can be easily lost, misplaced, or stolen.

Federal institutions reported 256 data breaches in the 2014 – 2015 fiscal year, up from 228 the year before — with accidental disclosure the leading cause. It marked the first time federal institutions were required to report breaches to the privacy commissioner. Previously, reporting was voluntary. Therrien's office undertook a special audit following concerns over a number of such data lapses, including a 2012 incident in which a portable hard drive containing the personal information of almost 600,000 student loan recipients went missing.

The audit, which examined practices at 17 federal institutions, identified a number of concerns:

- More than two-thirds of the agencies had not formally assessed the risks surrounding the use of all types of portable storage devices.

---

1 "2014–15 *Privacy Act* Annual Report to Parliament," Daniel Therrien, Office of the Privacy Commissioner of Canada, accessed March 2016. priv.gc.ca/information/ar/201415/201415_pa_e.asp

- More than 90 percent did not track all devices throughout their life cycle.

- One-quarter did not enforce the use of encrypted storage devices.

Therrien's annual report on private-sector organizations painted a similar picture.[2] Private entities are not legally required to report breaches to the privacy commissioner, but that will change when coming regulations flesh out a new law that imposes obligations on them.

Companies and other organizations will also have to notify affected people and relevant third parties in some circumstances about "breaches of security safeguards" that pose a "real risk of significant harm" to individuals, the commissioner's office says.[3] Organizations that knowingly fail to report breaches could face fines.

The concept of "significant harm" includes:

- Bodily harm.

- Humiliation.

- Damage to reputation or relationships.

- Loss of employment, business, or professional opportunities.

- Financial loss and identity theft.

In the United States, several federal laws contain security and breach notification provisions, while 47 states, the District of Columbia, and three territories also have laws on the books, according to a Congressional Research Service report.[4] It notes that the US system for policing breaches is also in transition, with a number of bills before Congress that could broaden existing provisions. New laws could also see an evolution in the enforcement duties of the Federal Trade Commission, responsible for consumer protection, and the Federal Communications Commission, which oversees telecommunications providers.

When you entrust public agencies and companies to handle your personal data with care, there is little you can do — beyond being prudent and thinking twice before sharing — to ensure privacy. However, there are steps that you can take to try to reduce the possibility of a privacy

2   "Privacy Protection: A Global Affair," Daniel Therrien, Office of the Privacy Commissioner of Canada, accessed March 2016. priv.gc.ca/information/ar/201415/2014_pipeda_e.asp
3   "The *Digital Privacy Act*: Summary of Key Changes to the *Personal Information and Electronic Documents Act*," Office of the Privacy Commissioner of Canada, accessed March 2016. priv.gc.ca/resource/fs-fi/02_05_d_63_s4_e.asp
4   "Data Security and Breach Notification Legislation: Selected Legal Issues," Alissa M. Dolan, Congressional Research Service, accessed March 2016. fas.org/sgp/crs/misc/R44326.pdf

breach, from securing devices to properly discarding sensitive information. In the Resources section at the end of this book, you will find web links for tips to protect personal information and reduce the likelihood of a privacy breach.

I. Identity Theft

Thieves attempting to steal personas are busier than ever. Identity theft is on the rise, and the numbers tell the story. The Canadian Anti-Fraud Centre received 8,465 ID theft complaints from January 1, 2015, to November 30, 2015. Even without the month of December, this represents a 20 percent increase compared to the previous year.[5]

The picture is the same in the United States. In 2014, there were 332,646 reported instances of identity theft compared to 290,099 the previous year, an increase of about 15 percent.[6]

The Federal Trade Commission also sounded the alarm about "impostor" scams, a category that witnessed the sharpest increase during the same 2013–to–2014 time period. These are scams where the crook pretends to be a legitimate authority such as an Internal Revenue Service official during tax season, or a lottery executive making false promises. The commission has vowed to "shut these scammers down."[7]

Identity fraud is the deceptive use of another person's identity information (e.g., to misuse a debit card or credit card). It doesn't matter whether the individual is dead or alive.

What do the crooks want? Their wish list includes the following information:

- Full name (first, middle, and last names).

- Date of birth (day, month, and year).

- Social Security Number or Social Insurance Number.

- Complete home address (unit number, building/house number, street/avenue, and zip or postal code).

---

5   "Monthly Summary Report — November 2015: Mass Marketing Fraud," Canadian Anti-Fraud Centre, accessed March 2016. antifraudcentre-centreantifraude.ca/reports-rapports/2015/nov-eng.htm
6   *Consumer Sentinel Network Data Book*, Federal Trade Commission, accessed March 2016. ftc.gov/system/files/documents/reports/consumer-sentinel-network-data-book-january-december-2014/sentinel-cy2014-1.pdf
7   "Identity Theft Tops FTC's Consumer Complaint Categories Again in 2014," Federal Trade Commission, accessed March 2016. ftc.gov/news-events/press-releases/2015/02/identity-theft-tops-ftcs-consumer-complaint-categories-again-2014

- Mother's maiden name.

- Usernames and passwords for online services.

- Driver's license number.

- Personal identification numbers (PINs).

- Credit card information (number, expiry date, and the three digits printed on the signature panel).

- Bank account numbers.

- Signature.

- Passport number.

Thieves can use your information to do the following:

- Access all your bank accounts.

- Open new bank accounts.

- Transfer bank balances.

- Apply for credit cards, loans, and other goods and services.

- Make purchases.

- Hide their own criminal activities.

- Obtain passports.

- Receive government benefits.

The Royal Canadian Mounted Police (RCMP) reports that identity theft can help facilitate organized criminal and terrorist activities, which seems to be a growing trend.[8]

1.1 What to do if you're a victim of identity theft

If you suspect you're a victim of identity theft, you may want to take the following steps:

- Contact the local police and file a report.

- Contact your bank or financial institution, and credit card company.

- Contact the two national credit bureaus TransUnion and Equifax.

---

8   "Identity Theft and Identity Fraud," Royal Canadian Mounted Police (RCMP), accessed March 2016. rcmp-grc.gc.ca/scams-fraudes/id-theft-vol-eng.htm

- In the US, contact the Federal Trade Commission (for identity theft) and the Federal Bureau of Investigation (for general fraud).

- In Canada, contact the Canadian Anti-Fraud Centre.

When making a report, you'll be asked to complete the following tasks:

- Ask the business to close the account.

- Ask the business to send you a letter confirming that the fraudulent account isn't yours, you aren't liable for it, and it was removed from your credit report.

Be sure to keep this letter, and use it if the account appears on your credit report. It's a good idea to write down whom you contacted and the date you communicated.

You also have the right to remove fraudulent information from your credit report, a process known as blocking. Once the information is blocked, it won't show up on your credit report, and companies can't try to collect the debt from you. If you have obtained an Identity Theft Report from the police, credit bureaus must honor your request to block this information. If you don't have a report, you still can dispute incorrect information in your credit file. It can take longer, and there's no guarantee that the credit bureaus will remove the information.

Prevention is one of the most effective tools to combat ID theft so consider the following best practices:

- Distrust any unsolicited emails, telephone calls, faxes, and mail attempting to convince you to hand over personal or financial information.

- Remove any identity documents you carry in your wallet or purse that you don't need and keep them in a secure place (e.g., safety deposit box, home safe).

- Regularly check your credit reports, bank statements, and credit card statements, and be sure to report anything out of the ordinary to the institutions, businesses, and credit bureaus.

- Swipe your card during a transaction rather than allowing a cashier to do it for you. If you must hand over your card, make sure that you can see it.

- Protect your personal identification number (PIN) when using an instant teller or a PIN pad.

- If your memory is up to the task, remember all personal identification numbers for payment cards and telephone calling cards, and avoid writing them on the cards.

- Know the billing cycles for your credit and debit cards.

- Shred personal and financial documents before tossing them in the garbage.

- Make sure you notify the post office and all relevant financial institutions (e.g., banks, credit card companies, utility companies) when you change your address.

2. Spam

Spam generally refers to the use of electronic messaging systems to send unsolicited, bulk messages. Spam can features malware, spyware, address-harvesters, or false or misleading representations made using email, social networking, or blogs. Typically the spam contains deceptive content, supports illegal activities, or serves as a pipeline for threats such as viruses.

Canada's anti-spam legislation makes it illegal for companies to install spam without consent on your laptop, smartphone, desktop, gaming console, or any other connected device, during the course of a commercial activity.

In the United States, it's up to individual states to draft their own laws to combat this online menace. Many states do allow consumers to take legal action.[9] Typically, the laws fall under the following general headings:

- Commercial emails and spam.

- Telemarketing and anti-solicitation.

- Anti-solicitation laws relating to texts and other emerging media.

- Unlawful trade practices.

- Pornography.

- Computer-related crime.

---

9 "US State Anti-Spam Laws: Introduction and Broader Framework," Cornell University Law School, accessed March 2016. law.cornell.edu/wex/inbox/state_anti-spam_laws

The content of a phishing email or text message is intended to convince you to act quickly to a false pretense or statement. Phishing messages usually ask you to "update," "validate," or "confirm" your account information or face dire consequences. The message or website includes official-looking logos and other identifying information. Government, financial institutions, and online payment services are common targets of brand spoofing.

You should be on the lookout for catchphrases such as "Email Money Transfer Alert: Please verify the payment information below … " Or, "It has come to our attention that your online banking profile needs to be updated as part of our continuous efforts to protect your account and reduce instances of fraud … " In some cases, the offending site can modify your browser address bar to make it look legitimate, including the web address of the real site and a secure "https://" prefix. See Sample 1.

What are the thieves after? They're trolling for personal information, including Social Security and Social Insurance numbers, full name, date of birth, full address, mother's maiden name, username, and passwords for online services. Phishing criminals can do a lot of damage, everything from accessing your financial accounts to applying for loans. So do yourself a favor and pay close attention.

2.1 What to do if you're a victim of phishing

If you suspect you're a victim of phishing, take the following steps:

- Contact the local police.

- Contact your financial institution and credit card company.

- Contact the two national credit bureaus TransUnion and Equifax and have fraud alerts placed on your credit reports.

- In the US, contact the Department of Health and Human Services Office of the Inspector General (for health-care and Medicare/Medicaid fraud), the Federal Bureau of Investigation (for general fraud), or the Internet Crime Complaint Center (for Internet fraud and online lottery/sweepstakes fraud).

- In Canada, contact the Canadian Anti-Fraud Centre. You can also contact the Spam Reporting Centre, which gathers information that helps the government to enforce the law.

The following are some tips to protect yourself:

- Don't trust any email or text message containing urgent requests for financial or personal information. Note that financial institutions and credit card companies will not use email to confirm an existing client's information.

- Call the organization, but make sure you use a telephone number from a credible source (i.e., phone book or bill).

- Never email personal or financial information to anyone you do not know well or any business.

- Do not click embedded links in an email that claims to bring you to a secure site.

- Look at a website's address line to verify if it displays something different from the address mentioned in the email.

- Update your computer regularly with antivirus software, email filters, spyware filters, and firewall programs.

- Check your bank, debit, and credit card statements regularly to ensure that every transaction is legitimate.

PHISHING EMAIL

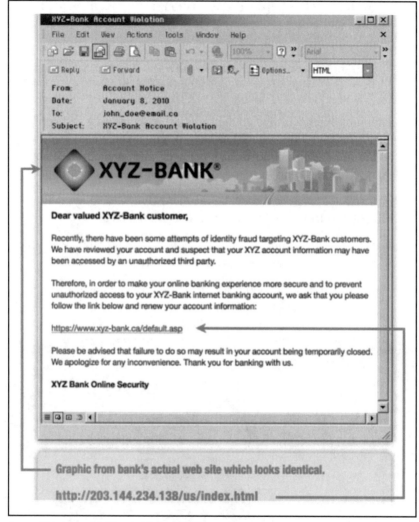

Source: Royal Canadian Mounted Police (RCMP),
E-mail Fraud/Phishing rcmp-grc.gc.ca/scams-fraudes/phishing-eng.htm

3. Targeted Advertising

I used to say that Google knows more about what I'm thinking of than my wife does. But that doesn't go far enough. Google knows more about what I'm thinking of than I do, because Google remembers all of it perfectly and forever.

— Bruce Schneier,
Data and Goliath: The Hidden Battles to Collect Your Data and Control Your World

Ever wonder why those online ads always seem to know if you're planning a trip, or buying a certain book? There is a reason. Companies mine your data in order to focus their advertising for the next time you might be in the mood to spend money.

It's one thing to be targeted because your online activity betrays a love of shoes. It's another thing to be targeted by a dieting service because of body-image concerns. How do these companies, institutions, and organizations do it? Cookies have a lot to do with it.

A cookie is a small file that your browser deposits on your computer's hard drive. Also known by the more ominous-sounding term, "persistent identifier," the cookie stores information about your interaction with the site that you've just visited. A website can later retrieve information such as login credentials and preferences that are stored on that cookie. Each cookie contains a unique number that allows that website to find your account.

But wait, it goes even further than that. Companies can now place their own cookies on pages belonging to other sites. These so-called third-party cookies track web users across many different sites, allowing ads to follow you around the web. "Research a particular car or vacation destination or medical condition, and for weeks you'll see ads for that car or city or a related pharmaceutical on every commercial Internet site you visit."[10]

There is also cookie-less tracking; that is, tracking your browsing habits using other methods. One such example involves so-called "web bugs," which are small image files that are placed on a web page or hidden in an email message. When you view the page or the message, the image is downloaded from a server, and this image can store detailed

---

10 *Data and Goliath: The Hidden Battles to Collect Your Data and Control Your World*, Bruce Schneier.

logs such as your location, Internet address, the page or message you were reading, and the date and time of your visit.

3.1 What to do to protect your browsing privacy

The Office of the Privacy Commissioner of Canada warns that protecting your privacy while browsing "is not an easy task," in large part because the default of web browsers is to store cookies indefinitely. Additionally, privacy tools can be difficult to find and challenging to use.

Setting up the browser to block cookies is easy enough. Simply go to the preferences or options section and select the "do not track" option. However, many websites that you visit force you to allow cookies to use their service, leaving consumers with the onerous task of allowing some cookies, but not others. If you configure your browser to delete stored cookies, this often only clears the traditional cookies we have described, not the other cookies that find innovative ways to avoid detection.

However, Christopher Parsons, a Postdoctoral Fellow at the Citizen Lab in the Munk School of Global Affairs at the University of Toronto, warns that there are all kinds of other cookies that end up on your hard drive, whether you want them or not.

"Consumers aren't just tracked by 'old-fashioned' cookies, but by flash cookies, perma-cookies, and more. And while flash cookies can be removed with some difficulty in your computer's flash settings, perma-cookies are just that: permanent. It involves your Internet provider actually changing the data you receive from websites, something that the consumer cannot themselves prevent or stop."

Some retailers, such as online apparel website Zappos, a unit of Amazon.com, give you the choice to opt out, as you can see in Sample 2.

However, it's clear from the explanation that selecting the "do not track" or "opt out" option doesn't get you entirely off the hook, in large part because as the notice explains, you can still be targeted by advertisers.

While the industry has been open to using techniques to warn consumers and give them opt-out provisions, there has been resistance to a general do-not-track policy that is akin to a do-not-call list that allows people to be avoid telemarketers by adding their names to a list.

Read the retailer's privacy policy: Companies don't always make this information easy to find. However, as with Zappos, you can usually find it by scrolling to the bottom of the page and clicking on a title

Sample 2
OPT-OUT FOR COOKIES

Zappos
POWERED by SERVICE™

Some People Prefer Rainbows, And Others Prefer Unicorns.

If you prefer not to see personalized ads, we totally get it. OPT OUT HERE. *

At Zappos.com, we know different people like different things, so we want our ads to reflect that.

That's why we love these ads! They display products that are relevant to you versus a typical ad that showcases a limited product offering.

Here's how it works:

These are the last products that you viewed on Zappos's website:

People who looked at these products often ended up choosing the following products:

Classic Tall Women's Boots
$164.95 » Go

Petty Women's Shoes
$135 » Go

Knowing this, we're able to create personalized ads for you. These ads feature some of the products you looked at on Zappos.com as well as some related products.

Importantly, no personal information of any kind was shared with any of the sites we advertise on. Everything is anonymous.

Now that you know more about how it works, if you still prefer not to see any personalized ads from Zappos, just click here. *

A company called Criteo helps Zappos to create these kinds of personalized ads. No personal information of any kind is shared with Criteo. You can learn more about Criteo and their privacy policies here.

* Please note that this opt-out relies on a cookie. If you delete all your cookies, we will no longer know that you have opted out.
If you want to block Criteo banners from your Internet browser, instructions are available here.

This opt-out only applies to the retargeting service provided by Criteo, and will not disable advertisements displayed by companies other than Criteo. Note: Other companies than Criteo offer this type of retargeting service. To learn more and know which companies currently display retargeted advertisement, click here.

Your status with Criteo is as follows:

You have an active cookie
You have not opted out
and have an active cookie from Criteo.

Source: Zappos.com

such as "Privacy Policy," where it explains what information is collected such as email, name, street address, postal code, telephone number, and password.

However, Christopher Parsons injects a word of caution, "These policies are often so general that they're meaningless; they will use 'may' instead of 'do,' and routinely fail to explicitly note all the kinds of information that is collected."

Activate your browser's "Do Not Track" option: For instance, when going into your Google Chrome's advanced settings and activating the Do Not Track option, you can learn more about the option from the pop-up box (see Sample 3).

GOOGLE CHROME'S DO NOT TRACK OPTION

Do Not Track   **✕**

Enabling "Do Not Track" means that a request will be included with your browsing traffic. Any effect depends on whether a website responds to the request, and how the request is interpreted. For example, some websites may respond to this request by showing you ads that aren't based on other websites you've visited. Many websites will still collect and use your browsing data; for example to improve security, to provide content, services, ads and recommendations on their websites, and to generate reporting statistics.

Learn more   [OK] [Cancel]

However, as you can see from the wording, there are no guarantees. Websites can, and do, ignore the request. Still, it's worth activating the option. If you're using the most recent version of Firefox, you can turn on Do Not Track by going into your preferences or options section and checking the box that says, "Tell sites that I do not want to be tracked" (see Sample 4).

Routinely remove individual cookies on your hard drive, to the extent that this is possible. In Microsoft Internet Explorer, you can go into the "Internet Options" portion of your menu and block cookies from all websites (see Sample 5).

Perhaps one of the best solutions is installing ad/tracking blockers to your browser. They block many cookies. Christopher Parsons suggests two popular ones:

- Ghostery.com

- AdBlockPlus.org

The installation instructions are simple, allowing you to complete the task in minutes. "In addition to letting you block the trackers," says Parsons, "you can also just see how many are working on any given site. Most you'll have never heard of!"

FIREFOX DO NOT TRACK OPTION

Parsons says that these kinds of ad-ons are invaluable because rather than politely asking an advertiser or website not to track you, you actually *prevent* the tracking from occurring in the first place. While such tools don't prevent the more pernicious kinds of surveillance based on flash cookies, perma-cookies, or other techniques discussed earlier, they are the best means of stopping old-fashioned, cookie-based surveillance.

"And all it takes is a few clicks, and your web experience is changed from one of persistent tracking and surveillance to one of far fewer ads and distractions," says Parsons.

MICROSOFT INTERNET EXPLORER
INTERNET OPTIONS

Internet Options ? X

| General | Security | **Privacy** | Content | Connections | Programs | Advanced |

Settings

Select a setting for the Internet zone.

Block All Cookies

- Blocks all cookies from all websites
- Cookies that are already on this computer cannot be read by websites

| Sites | Import | Advanced | Default |

Pop-up Blocker

Prevent most pop-up windows from appearing.   **Settings**

☑ Turn on Pop-up Blocker

InPrivate

☐ Do not collect data for use by InPrivate Filtering

☑ Disable toolbars and extensions when InPrivate Browsing starts

| OK | Cancel | Apply |

- **Log off when not using social media**: Sign out of Facebook, Twitter, and other social networking accounts if you're not on the given company's website. Facebook and others have historically tracked individuals by logging when they visit sites with a "Like" button. It doesn't matter that you didn't like the article or page, you may still be tracked by the company!

- **Clean house regularly**: Empty your "normal" cookies. This can force a company to start over to develop a profile on you when it relies on cookies that you can delete right from your web browser.

- **Erase your history on a regular basis**: Your Internet history, along with other kinds of data that are harder or almost impossible to "scrub away," can be used to fingerprint your web browser. In effect, it means that you could be tracked without ever putting a tracking cookie on your computer! Erasing your history makes that a bit harder, though it doesn't entirely prevent such tracking.

- **Seek and destroy those flash cookies**: Where possible, find and delete your "flash" cookies. When you see animated video on the web, it often uses a technology called flash. The same technology can also be used to drop tracking cookies on your computer, which can remain when you delete the cookies from your web browser. You can often delete such flash cookies in the settings for flash that are on your computer, though the location of those settings varies based on your operating system.

Note: All of these tips are predominantly for desktop computers. It's a lot harder to limit tracking on mobile devices.

4. Social Media

"Sometimes data we only intend to share with a few becomes surveillance data for the world."

— Bruce Schneier, *Data and Goliath: The Hidden Battles to Collect Your Data and Control Your World*

Much of the information we share can be found on social networking sites such as Facebook, LinkedIn, and Twitter, which allow individuals to form online social communities.

Users create profiles that include personal data such as their contact information, gender, political and religious beliefs, relationship status, and interests. These biographies can also include pictures, videos, and music. However, it goes even further than that. Users also describe the connections that they have with others, which are typically based on common interests, backgrounds, and hobbies. Venues such as public or private messaging, file-sharing, and discussion boards keep the conversation going.

While these social media sites provide wonderful opportunities to share content, keep in touch with friends and family, discover long-lost friends and acquaintances and make new connections, it is important to be cautious when clicking on links and sharing information. For instance, be aware that those slightly embarrassing party pictures you posted online could come back to haunt you when searching for a job. Indeed, this is the kind of "reputational" risk that concerns the Office of the Privacy Commissioner of Canada, which has announced a five-year commitment to study the "risks stemming from the vast amount of personal information posted online and on existing and potential mechanisms for managing these risks."

The privacy commissioner references the work of American social media scholar and Microsoft Principal Researcher Danah Boyd (http://www.danah.org/) who characterizes the information posted online as having four "distinct features." 1) Online information is persistent in that deleting once it has been uploaded can be challenging, if not impossible; 2) Online information can be replicated; 3) It has the potential to be visible to a vast and unintended audience; 4) And it can be accessed through a search function.[11]

Though it is always wise to read each social network's privacy policies, Microsoft has drafted some useful tips.

---

11 "Online Reputation: What are they saying about me? Discussion", Paper prepared by the Policy and Research Group of the Office of the Privacy Commissioner of Canada, 2016, pp.3-4, https://www.priv.gc.ca/information/research-recherche/2016/or_201601_e.pdf

Microsoft's 11 Tips for Social Networking Safety[12]

1. Be careful when clicking links in messages you receive from friends on your social website. Though the links may appear legitimate, they could be fakes. This is because fraudsters can perpetrate the kind of identity theft we've discussed earlier in this chapter. So take precautionary measures such as hovering your cursor over the link to see the address. Or, make sure the spelling of the words on the link matches what you expect to see.

2. Remember key details that you've posted about yourself. In large part, this is because hackers typically click on the "Forgot your password?" link on a website's account login page. Then, to break into your actual account, they search for answers to security questions such as your favourite colour, pet's name or mother's middle name. In short, the kind of information that we readily share on social networking sites. So if the website allows it, avoid drawing from easily searchable material when setting up passwords and answers to security questions.

3. Be cautious when receiving messages from friends. Hackers can, and do, break into accounts to send messages that look like they're coming from people you know. If you have doubts, simply take a few moments and find another way to contact your friend.

4. Do not allow social networking services to scan your email address book without finding out why they want to do this.

5. Type your social networking site's URL directly into your browser, or simply bookmark it. By clicking a link to your website through email or another website, you might be inadvertently divulging your account and password to a bogus website.

6. Be selective about who you accept as a friend. Identity thieves can create fake profiles.

7. Choose your social network carefully by reading and understanding its privacy policy, which should be clearly explained in the kind of easy-to-understand language that privacy regulators are advising companies to use.

---

12 11 tips for social networking safety, Microsoft, https://www.microsoft.com/en-us/safety/online-privacy/social-networking.aspx

8. Assume that everything you post on a social networking site is permanent, even if it may be deleted from a search engine, or your website.

9. Be careful when downloading third-party plug-ins, which crooks can use to steal personal information.

10. For the reasons already discussed in this tip sheet, think twice before using social networking sites at work.

11. If you're a parent, talk to your children about how they use social networking sites.

Top ten popular social networking sites[13]
May 2016

Site	Number of monthly visits
1. Facebook	1,100,000,000
2. Twitter	310,000,000
3. LinkedIn	255,000,000
4. Pinterest	250,000,000
5. Google Plus +	250,000,000
6. Tumblr	110,000,000
7. Instagram	100,000,000
8. VK	80,000,000
9. Flickr	65,000,000
10. Vine	42,000,000

13 The eBusiness Guide, http://www.ebizmba.com/articles/social-networking-websites

Ten most popular file sharing websites May 2016[14]

Site	Estimated unique monthly visits
1. Dropbox	35,000,000
2. MediaFire	22,500,000
3. 4Shared	21,000,000
4. Google Drive	18,500,000
5. SkyDrive	16,000,000
6. iCloud	9,500,000
7. Box	6,750,000
8. Mega	6,500,000
9. ZippyShare	6,250,000
10. Uploaded	6,000,000

Most social networking websites make their money from advertisers. They are attracted to the wealth of personal information, allowing for highly targeted advertising. For example, Facebook allows advertisers to search by criteria: location, sex, age, education status, workplace, political views, interests, relationship status, and keyword. For their part, advertisers on LinkedIn target ads by industry, seniority, job function, company size, geography, number of connections, and gender.

The House of Commons committee that studied this issue produced a report on April 13, 2013, called *Privacy and Social Media in the Age of Big Data*. The discussion provided a valuable window into the debate about the complex issues that regulators in Canada, the United States, and Europe face when juggling privacy concerns with legitimate commercial interests. The committee heard many witnesses speak about the need to strike a balance between social media companies' desire to innovate and experiment with new products and services, and the appropriate level of protection for personal information.[15]

---

14 eBusiness Guide, http://www.ebizmba.com/articles/file-sharing-websites
15 *Privacy and Social Media in the Age of Big Data,* Pierre-Luc Dusseault, MP Chair, House of Commons, accessed February 2016. parl.gc.ca/content/hoc/Committee/411/ETHI/Reports/RP6094136/ethirp05/ethirp05-e.pdf

5. Technology

Hackers are only as sophisticated as they have to be. And the majority of compromises are targets of opportunity. It's a little bit like trying to avoid being robbed, or having your car broken into. All you need to do is take a few basic precautions and make it easier for the criminal to go on to the next guy.

— Eva Galperin, Global Policy Analyst,
Electronic Frontier Foundation (ssd.eff.org/en)

In our increasingly wired world, hackers and scam artists are always on the hunt for new victims. While it's important to resist being paranoid, taking basic safety precautions is the wise approach. As Eva Galperin correctly suggests, avoid making yourself an easy target.

Typically, the most reputable commercial organizations and institutions do a good job of protecting your online activities such as banking and shopping. However, there's a range of everyday activity such as regular email correspondence and web-surfing that should also be protected. Galperin co-authored the *Surveillance Self-Defense* guide for the San Francisco-based Electronic Frontier Foundation. The guide is a tip sheet on ways of making your online communication safer, whether using a computer, mobile phone, or tablet. The guide provides a basic checklist that people should consider in relation to security.

When conducting an assessment, there are five main questions you should ask yourself to keep your data secure:[16]

1. What do you want to protect? (This is usually information; for example, emails, contact lists, instant messages, devices, and files.)

2. Who do you want to protect it from?

3. How likely is it that you will need to protect it?

4. How bad are the consequences if you fail?

5. How much trouble are you willing to go through in order to try to prevent a data breach?

---

16 "When Conducting an Assessment, There Are Five Main Questions You Should Ask Yourself," Eva Galperin, *Surveillance Self-Defense*, Electronic Frontier Foundation, accessed March 2016. ssd.eff.org/en/module/introduction-threat-modeling

5.1 Encryption

It is a good idea to encrypt your email and data – that is, make it unreadable to prying eyes. Encryption stems from the Greek word kryptos, meaning hidden or secret. There are three key elements to consider in the digital sphere:

- Securing your Internet connection.

- Shielding your messages in transit.

- Safeguarding data stored on your computer or mobile device.

A wide range of tools and services can help you carry out these tasks — some free or built into programs or hardware, others for a fee. Sometimes they work in tandem to provide you with greater protection than they would alone.

Start with your browser – if the web address for your email provider begins with HTTPS — Hypertext Transfer Protocol, or HTTP, with an S (for secure) and possibly a tiny padlock in the address bar, then encryption is enabled. It means your browser and the site server are working together to keep snoopers — say, someone using the same public Wi-Fi connection – from stealing your login credentials.

As *Wired* magazine noted,[17] HTTPS was once used chiefly to protect login pages and shopping and banking sites, but web administrators are incorporating it into many other kinds of pages, such as social media and government sites.

The free Tor[18] service allows you to browse online in anonymity by masking your Internet Protocol (IP) address, a sort of digital fingerprint that can reveal your location and personal interests. The indiscretions of David Petraeus — the Central Intelligence Agency director who resigned over an extramarital affair — came to light after the Federal Bureau of Investigation used IP addresses to trace harassing emails his mistress had sent to another woman.

The Electronic Frontier Foundation has produced a helpful graphic showing the benefits of using HTTPS and Tor together.[19]

In the same vein as Tor, a number of commercial outfits provide what's known as a Virtual Private Network, allowing you online privacy as well

17 https://www.wired.com/2016/04/hacker-lexicon-what-is-https-encryption/
18 https://www.torproject.org
19 https://www.eff.org/pages/tor-and-https

as Wi-Fi security. Hotspot Shield offers a free, basic service as well as a premium package.

Email encryption has gained popularity amid concern about prying eyes in cyberspace.

A highly secure option is Pretty Good Privacy (PGP) available free in the form of the Gnu Privacy Guard, or GnuPG. The program allows you to encrypt your messages. It involves creation of a public key, a string of characters you provide to others, as well as a private key you must closely guard. You can send encrypted messages to others as long as you know their public key.

PGP can also be used to apply a digital signature to a public message as a means of verifying that it came from you.

The widely used Microsoft Outlook email program provides a means of encrypting messages,[20] but it requires sender and recipient to first exchange digital signatures. Technophobes and impatient users may find such options challenging, but given the current concerns about email security, several user-friendly services now offer enhanced protection. A couple of well-reviewed ones that offer free packages are ProtonMail and Tutanota.

However, encryption purists point out that because a third party – the email provider – is involved, the user cannot be entirely certain of absolute security with such services.

The messaging service Whatsapp, owned by Facebook, and Apple's iMessage also feature encryption.

In addition, it is generally getting easier to encrypt stored messages and files. It's best to encrypt all of your data, not just a few folders. Most computers and smartphones offer complete, full-disk encryption as an option. Android offers it under its "Security" settings. Apple devices such as the iPhone and iPad describe it as "Data Protection" and turn it on if you set a passcode. On computers that run Windows Pro, it's known as BitLocker.

If you have the standard version of Windows, you can use a free program called DiskCryptor. On Macs it's called FileVault. On Linux distributions, full-disk encryption is usually offered when you first set up your system.

---

20 https://support.office.com/en-us/article/Encrypt-e-mail-messages-84d7e382-5f76-4d71-8705-324489b710a2

5.2 Passwords

Passwords became big news when it emerged in late 2015 that the US Federal Bureau of Investigation had obtained a court order to crack the password of the iPhone belonging to terror suspect Syed Rizwan Farook. The FBI said that Farook and his wife Tashfeen Malik tried to "conceal and destroy electronic evidence before they were killed in a shootout with police."[21]

Fourteen people were killed and another 21 were injured in the mass shooting in San Bernardino, California. Defying the court order, Apple rebuffed the FBI's demand to allow it to crack the password. [22]

But the FBI persisted.

"We simply want the chance, with a search warrant, to try to guess the terrorist's passcode without the phone essentially self-destructing and without it taking a decade to guess correctly. That's it," wrote FBI director James Comey in a news release.

"We don't want to break anyone's encryption or set a master key loose on the land. I hope thoughtful people will take the time to understand that. Maybe the phone holds the clue to finding more terrorists. Maybe it doesn't. But we can't look the survivors in the eye, or ourselves in the mirror, if we don't follow this lead."[23]

However, executive director of Ryerson University's Privacy and Big Data Institute, Ann Cavoukian, took a less charitable view of the FBI's encryption-busting request.

"Make no mistake: Building a back door into the San Bernardino iPhone to access encrypted data would build a back door into all iPhones of a similar model. The operating system software is essentially the same; thus, opening one iPhone to access personal data would open all others. And once the back door has been built, it would be available not only to the U.S. government, but foreign governments and criminal hackers around the world."[24]

---

21 "FBI Will Investigate San Bernardino Shootings as Terrorist Act," Federal Bureau of Investigation (FBI), accessed May 2016. fbi.gov/news/news_blog/fbi-will-investigate-san-bernardino-shootings-as-terrorist-act
22 "Answers to Your Questions about Apple and Security," Apple, accessed May 2016. apple.com/customer-letter/answers
23 "FBI Director Comments on San Bernardino Matter," Federal Bureau of Investigation (FBI), accessed May 2016. fbi.gov/news/pressrel/press-releases/fbi-director-comments-on-san-bernardino-matter
24 "The Price Is too High: Apple Must Not Give in to FBI demands," Ann Cavoukian, The Globe and Mail, accessed May 2016. theglobeandmail.com/opinion/encryption-is-vital-to-protect-our-rights-in-a-digital-world/article28791923

This debate illustrates the importance of robust passwords.

The Electronic Frontier Foundation suggests that a really strong password will be longer than 15 characters. Here are some password tips from Public Safety Canada:[25]

- Make sure it's a minimum length of eight characters.

- Use a combination of upper and lower case letters and at least one number.

- Include at least one character that isn't a letter or number.

- Be creative. Use the first letter of each word of a memorable sentence or phrase, then make it even tougher by changing some of the letters to numbers (e.g. use a "3" to replace an "e").

- Try a mix of your pet's name, your favourite numbers, the street you grew up on or other combinations.

- Stay away from things like words spelled backwards, misspelled words, and abbreviations that are easy to figure out.

- Don't repeat numbers (5555) and letters (bbbb), include simple sequences (abcdefg or 56789) or use letters that appear in a row on your keyboard (qwerty).

- Never use your name, birthday, driver's license or passport number.

- Don't store them on your computer or in your mobile phone.

- Change your passwords often.

- Clear your browsing history or cache after online banking and shopping.

- If you get an email that includes a password you've just set up, delete it.

- Make sure that you change your smartphone's original default password.

- Change your passwords after implementing a fix or following an attempted breach.

- Use different passwords for different online accounts, especially those dealing with sensitive information or financial data. (See additional tips in the Online banking section.)

25 http://www.getcybersafe.gc.ca/cnt/prtct-yrslf/prtctn-dntty/usng-psswrds-en.aspx

Unless you have a photographic memory, choosing and remembering hacker-resistant passwords can be challenging, if not impossible. Fortunately, there are tools to make the task easier. For instance, a password manager, also known as a password safe, is a software tool that protects all your passwords by keeping them in a secure location, either on your computer's hard drive or a USB drive. The password manager can handle the entire process of creating and remembering the passwords. This means that you only have to remember one password in order to get into the safe that contains all the others.

To invent a truly random password that you'll actually be able to remember, the Electronic Frontier Foundation suggests using Arnold G. Reinhold's Diceware technique (world.std.com/~reinhold/diceware. html), which is a method of choosing a secure password using dice and a list of Diceware words. For example, using five random words (64 bits) is believed to help protect against a criminal attacker, while relying on six random words (77 bits) is believed to help protect against all but the most motivated state-level attackers such as the US's powerful National Security Agency.

Nowhere is security more important as when conducting business online such as shopping or banking. Though reputable companies like Amazon and banks in North America have the kinds of secure and encrypted sites discussed earlier in this chapter, it's prudent to take some time to think a bit more seriously about security.

When you are asked to set up a password upon creating a new account, make sure you take the kinds of precautions we've already discussed. Use complex passwords. Change them frequently.

Before sharing personal or financial information online, confirm that the final payment web page for your purchase is protected with encryption.

Security features are different for every web browser, so it's wise to take the time to learn the basics for the one you prefer to use. The two most common signs of a secure page for any browser are:

- The web address begins with Hypertext Transfer Protocol Secure, or HTTPS, discussed earlier, which is the protocol used to access a secure Web server. The https is the prefix of the web address. (for example, https://www.nameofshop.com).

- To the left of the prefix is a padlock symbol that you can click for the security information, as shown in the illustration that follows.

An increasing number of public places such as coffee shops and bookstores provide free Wi-Fi connections. Making connections on your tablet, mobile phone, or laptop while sipping a cup of coffee or reading a good book has never been easier, but a note of caution is needed. Authorities such as the Ontario Ministry of Government and Consumer Services recommend against doing your online shopping or banking from these locations, mainly because they do not offer adequate security measures. "A strong password-protected connection at home is your best bet for safer shopping."[26]

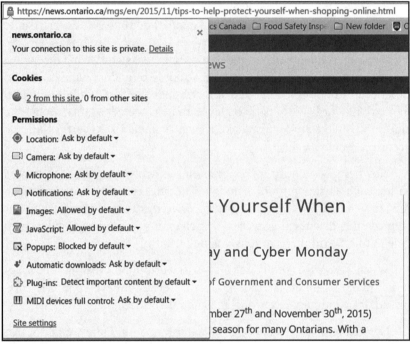

Ontario Ministry of Government and Consumer Services Website

8 Tips for Holiday Shopping Online[27]

- Use complex and different passwords on the websites you use for shopping.

- Enter personal information only on reputable websites with "https" or a lock in the address bar.

- Update or install Internet security software.

---

26 Ontario Ministry of Government and Consumer Services
27 8 Tips for Holiday Shopping Online, Office of the Information and Privacy Commissioner of Alberta, November 27, 2015

Pay Safe

- Use a secure home network when shopping or checking bank statements. Free Wi-Fi can't be trusted.

- Ensure fraud protection is in place if using a third-party payment provider.

Buyers Be Aware

- Follow up with the retailer if you don't receive an email confirming your purchase.

- If the deal sounds unbelievable, it probably is, so don't click on those links you find in email or on social media, and don't reply to text messages or provide information over the phone.

- Phishing emails bait you to share information. Email like this may appear to be coming from a trusted source, but reputable businesses don't ask for your personal information via email.

Information technology expert David Papp's quick fraud awareness tips to remember when online shopping:[28]

1. The best way to get your attention is with a "stunning" price, so be wary of things that are too good to be true.

2. The best scams don't look like scams, they tend to be "time" sensitive with "limited" time offers. The idea is to get you to act right away.

3. Usually the scammers don't get reviews.

4. Safe payment systems take hard work, and a new website might not have put in the effort.

5. Look for a "real" owner.

6. Security protects your connection, but doesn't protect you from who you connect to.

7. Review your online account settings.

8. Keep personal information personal.

---

28 Global Edmonton, Online shopping tips, http://davidpapp.com/2015/11/23/online-shopping-tips/

9. Ensure the website address makes sense.

10. Consider a low-limit credit card. That way even if someone finds out about it, the crook can't go and "have fun with it."

5.3 Online banking[29]

It's important to use the same precautions when banking online. Like reputable retailers, banks in North America use sophisticated technology and layers of security to help protect customers from fraud when doing their banking online or using a mobile banking app. Still, you bear a degree of responsibility to make sure that transactions are conducted safely.

What follows are simple steps that the Canadian Bankers Association suggests you can take in addition to the tips we've already discussed:

- Guard against malicious software by installing anti-virus, anti-spyware and Internet firewall tools on all your devices. Keep them active and updated.

- Only download apps directly from your bank or a reputable app store that your bank directs you to. Crooks create "legitimate" looking apps that steal your personal and financial information.

- Never send personal or financial information by email.

- As we have stressed, make sure that your passwords are difficult for criminals to guess. Use a combination of upper- and lower-case letters, numbers and symbols when creating a password, and make sure it is a password you will remember. Common weak passwords include:

  - Your name or a family member's name.

  - Your birthdate, phone number or address, or that of a family member.

  - Your account or bank card number.

  - Any word or number that would be easy to guess.

  - A password you've used for other websites.

- Always choose a unique password for all online banking and credit card accounts and change the password regularly.

29 Source: How to Bank Safely Online, Canadian Bankers Association, Feb. 26, 2016, http://www.cba.ca/en/consumer-information/42-safeguarding-your-money/743-how-to-bank-safely-online

- If something's not right, contact your bank.

- Although your bank may contact you by text, email, and phone, it will never ask you to disclose personal information such as your credit card number, PIN or online banking password because it already has that information.

- Always review your transactions online to ensure that they're legitimate. If you see anything suspicious, contact your bank immediately.

- The Canadian Bankers Association also publishes information online at cba.ca/en/consumer-information/42-safeguarding-your-money/481-cba-fraud-prevention-tip.

6. Transparency Reports

Demand more of the companies we interact with. Don't buy their "protecting your privacy is our priority" myth and demand more from them. Complain. When you have the ability to choose, which is increasingly less so, choose those who genuinely do protect you. Don't buy new services until you know what is going on.

— Gus Hosein,
Executive Director of Privacy International

Public concern about telecommunications and Internet providers handing information to police and spy agencies has prompted companies to publish transparency reports. The demand for more openness was fueled by leaks from former American intelligence contractor Edward Snowden, whose significant disclosures revealed the US National Security Agency had access to a huge volume of telecommunications data.

Transparency reports — regularly produced by Facebook, Twitter, Apple, Rogers, Comcast, and others — generally detail the number of requests received from agencies in specific countries.

The report may also tell you something about the nature of the request (e.g., subpoena, court order, warrant), the sort of information being sought (e.g., content, transaction data, subscriber information), whether the company rejected (or objected to) disclosure, and whether notice was provided to the account holder.

However, the existing system is a patchwork, with some companies proving more forthcoming than others. For instance, we know that in

Canada from January 1 to June 30, 2015, Twitter received 35 government requests for account information, and that it complied in whole or in part in 63 percent of these cases, but little more.[30]

In comparison, file-sharing service Dropbox provides a more detailed breakdown of the types of requests it receives — including those related to national security.[31] Still, due to legal restrictions Dropbox could report only that it received between 0 and 249 security-related requests in the first half of 2015 — nothing more precise.

Canadian officials have been fretting, too. A senior Public Safety employee warned her deputy minister in 2014 that the move by telecommunications firms to be more open with the public about their role in police and spy surveillance could divulge "sensitive operational details."[32] Industry Canada has since published guidelines as to what companies should and should not include in their transparency reports.

Gus Hosein, Executive Director of London-based Privacy International, would like to see a wider range of firms reporting. "I hope to see transparency reports from electricity companies in the future as they get requests for our personal information, information about our activities, how many people are in our homes, and what kinds of devices we are using."

Some argue that even when companies disclose as much as possible, it really only provides a broad-brush statistical snapshot of government demands for user information.

The US and Canadian governments do publish annual statistics on court-approved wiretaps. However, there have been calls for more systematic government reporting of other kinds of data collection.

In Canada, federal Privacy Commissioner Daniel Therrien has expressed disappointment that the RCMP has not divulged more about the requests it makes to communication providers.

"I note that not much progress has been made on that issue," Therrien said in an interview with The Canadian Press. He has also pointed out that most of the newer surveillance powers in the Criminal Code — such as orders to companies to produce data and police use of location-tracking techniques — have not been reported on.

---

30 "Information Requests (Canada)," Twitter Transparency Report, accessed March 2016. transparency.twitter.com/country/ca
31 "2015 Transparency Report," Dropbox, accessed March 2016. dropbox.com/transparency
32 "Disclosure of 'Sensitive' Telecom Surveillance Details Worried Feds: Memo," Jim Bronskill, *The Globe and Mail*, accessed March 2016. theglobeandmail.com/news/national/disclosure-of-sensitive-telecom-surveillance-details-worried-feds-memo/article21839258

5
Traveling

Voyages across oceans and borders have long been recorded, as any genealogist who has spotted her grandfather's name on a steamship passenger list can tell you. But modern technologies have given government agencies new and extensive means to monitor, record, and analyze our global movements. And the mini-computers in our pockets and embedded in our vehicles mean that even a trip to the corner store may not be an entirely private journey. Increasingly, we are inviting others along for the ride, whether we know it or not.

I. Smartphones

Smartphones have become more popular due to the release of devices that sell for less than $200, discounted by carriers who subsidize the price for users who sign up for wireless contracts. The devices are also popular because of downloadable apps that perform an impressive and ever-expanding array of tasks. Examples include consulting a traffic app on the commute to work, loading retail coupons, and streaming television programs.

The more consumers use their mobile devices for broader and deeper purposes, the greater the risk of exposing their personal information. Perhaps even more concerning, there is evidence to suggest that many apps collect information that isn't actually needed to provide the service. Reports of popular apps collecting irrelevant information or transmitting data when devices are turned off has led to significant backlash.

The following are some tips on how to make your private information more secure:

- Use a password to protect access to your smartphone.

- Add a tracking service that enables the device to be wiped remotely because once the bad guys have the hardware, it's very difficult to keep them out.

- Back up all the personal data on your device, including photos and email, then delete anything you don't really need.

- Keep the number of apps to a minimum.

- Try to avoid giving apps unnecessary permissions. Remember, an app would never ask for permission unless it needed it, and at that point, you are in the best position to decide if you want to grant it. Check permissions during the life of the app.

- During installation, verify that the permissions being sought by the mobile applications match not only what the privacy policy says, but also what you would expect the app to require. Permissions within mobile apps access your device's data and capabilities in order to run. These permissions could include location, identity, email, and contacts.

- Download apps from reputable sites such as Google Play, Apple, or Microsoft. Keep an eye open for dodgy-looking apps with names that are almost, but not quite, the ones you want.

- Check the developer's privacy policy to see whether it tells you what personal information the app will be accessing, and how it may be used or disclosed. If you can't locate the privacy policy, or any privacy information for that matter, consider whether it's worth taking the risk of downloading the app. Many mobile applications lack the most basic and minimal building blocks for privacy protection.

- Keep your apps up to date and regularly delete the ones you no longer want or use. An out-of-date app can provide hackers the opening they crave to do their nasty work.

Though the explosion of apps makes identifying the most trendy a potentially perilous exercise, we will examine one — Snapchat — that has attracted attention due to both popularity and controversy. Part of the interest here is the crossover nature of some applications. Yes, it's a phone-based application — an "app" — but, by its very nature, it is social media. These blurred lines can create entirely new security and privacy concerns.

Snapchat is a text, video and photo-based messaging application for mobile phones. Founded in 2012, the company is based in Venice, California.[1]

It boasts more than 100 million "daily active Snapchatters" and is growing. Users skew towards the young.

Snapchat's "twist" is that the text, photos and videos you share disappear shortly after being viewed by the person at the other end who is usually a "friend." The time period depends on the user. It can be one second, 10 seconds, or longer.

In addition to running on mobile phones, the app also lives on the iPad, Android tablets and iPod touch, which are often used by young children, a problem we'll discuss a little later in this section.

According to the Silicon Valley, California-based organization ConnectSafely.org, Snapchat was developed as an "antidote" to the more traditional social networking services such as Facebook, where media that you post can live forever and people have to worry about their reputations. "Snapchat users feel like they don't have to worry if they're having a bad hair day or just want to make a silly face."[2]

However, as with anything we share in cyberspace, there are risks. And this has been the case with Snapchat in both the United States and Canada. For example, an investigation by The Canadian Press discovered that third-party accounts were posting Snapchat pictures showing questionable behavior at universities.

"They are images of dormitory drug use, drunken debauchery and naked selfies — captured by self-destructing photo apps such as Snapchat.

"But social media images intended to be fleeting, and for a limited group of friends, are taking on a longer life and a much larger audience through unsanctioned accounts that collect posts from students and repost them to anyone who subscribes.

---

1 Company Overview of Snapchat, Inc., http://www.bloomberg.com/research/stocks/private/snapshot.asp?privcapId=224055283
2 "A Parent's Guide to Snapchat", ConnectSafely.org, 2013, p. 3, http://www.connectsafely.org/wp-content/uploads/snapchat_guide.pdf

"The accounts raise questions about child pornography, revenge porn and invasions of privacy, because people in the background of photos and videos featured in these rogue accounts may not have consented to the post being shown to a wider audience. These accounts have cropped up at least 26 universities and colleges across the country, according to an analysis by The Canadian Press."[3]

Though Snapchat's ephemeral images are only to be shared among friends, they may be given a longer shelf-life, allowing them to be distributed.

How is this done? Well, images and videos only meant to last a few seconds can actually be captured, either by a smartphone's operating system that allows someone to capture what's on the screen, by a third-party app that allows the capture of videos, or by another mobile device that simply records the videos.

As well, Snapchat has come under fire from the U.S. Federal Trade Commission which said that it "deceived consumers with promises about the disappearing nature of messages sent through the service." The commission issued a news release to announce that Snapchat had dealt with its concerns, allowing the two sides to reach an agreement.[4]

On the same day that the commission issued its news release, Snapchat took to its blog to tell its side of the story in which it admitted no wrongdoing, and instead insisted that it merely needed to communicate its privacy policy more clearly.

"When we started building Snapchat, we were focused on developing a unique, fast, and fun way to communicate with photos. We learned a lot during those early days. One of the ways we learned was by making mistakes, acknowledging them, and fixing them.

"While we were focused on building, some things didn't get the attention they could have. One of those was being more precise with how we communicated with the Snapchat community. This morning we entered into a consent decree with the FTC that addresses concerns raised by the commission. Even before today's consent decree was announced, we had resolved most of those concerns over the past year by improving the

---

3   Adina Bresge, "Snapchat pictures re-posted by 3rd party accounts showcase debauchery at universities: 'This is likely promoting all kinds of serious invasions of privacy'", The Canadian Press, April 26, 2016, http://www.cbc.ca/beta/news/canada/nova-scotia/snapchat-university-debauchery-1.3553109
4   The Federal Trade Commission, Snapchat Settles FTC Charges That Promises of Disappearing Messages Were False, May 8, 2014, https://www.ftc.gov/news-events/press-releases/2014/05/snapchat-settles-ftc-charges-promises-disappearing-messages-were

wording of our privacy policy, app description, and in-app just-in-time notifications. And we continue to invest heavily in security and counter-measures to prevent abuse.

"We are devoted to promoting user privacy and giving Snapchatters control over how and with whom they communicate. That's something we've always taken seriously, and always will."[5]

There are lessons to be learned from these examples. Although the text messages, photos, and videos are only meant to be shared by a select few, they can live forever.

It is for this reason that the Office of the Privacy Commissioner of Canada has commissioned a study to examine ways teenagers between the ages of 12 to 16 use Snapchat.

"The research will shed light on the steps that youth take in making their decisions, the outside factors that influence their decisions, and whether demographic factors, such as age and gender, have an impact on their decision making process. The results will be useful for improving public and parent knowledge around privacy, creating educational interventions relating to privacy, and providing guidance to industry about best practices for handling young people's content and data."[6]

The research project is scheduled to be completed by the end of March 2017.

While there is a need for more study, organizations such as Connect-Safely.org provide basic tips for ensuring privacy:

1. **Manage your settings:** If you don't want just anybody sending you photos or videos, make sure that you're using the default setting to only accept incoming pictures from "My Friends."

2. **Screen capture is possible:** It's a good idea to remind teens to avoid sending embarrassing pictures and videos. Although Snapchat lets you know if your message has been opened and saved, there are instances when you may be in the dark. For example, you'll never know if someone has used another mobile device camera or recorder to capture the image or photo that you've sent.

3. **Don't screen-capture without permission:** If someone has shared a photo with you, ask if it's OK if you save it.

5   Snapchat Blog.com, Our Agreement with the FTC, May 8, 2014, http://snapchat-blog.com/post/85132301440/our-agreement-with-the-ftc
6   The Office of the Privacy Commissioner of Canada, Project Descriptions Contributions Program 2016-2017, April 16, 2016, https://www.priv.gc.ca/resource/cp/2016-2017/cp_bg_e.asp

4. **Protect your password:** Ensure that your password is strong and unique. Parents should remind their kids to avoid sharing passwords, even with people they consider to be their best friends.

5. **Keeping it real:** Though Snapchat doesn't allow users to search for new friends, there are still ways to find people you don't know by locating their Snapchat username on other services, and then adding them to your friends list.

6. **Sexting concerns:** Parents should worry about kids sending naked or sexually explicit pictures of themselves. It's best to insist that teens never take or distribute images that could get them into trouble.

7. **Block the user:** If you're receiving unwanted snaps, use the Snapchat settings that allow you to block certain individuals. Tap on the "menu" button, and then "My Friends." Swipe across their name on Apple devices, or on Android phones, press and hold the person's name. Finally, press "Edit," and then "Block" or "Delete."

8. **Flag underage users:** Anyone under 13 years of age is not supposed to be using Snapchat. If you're concerned that this is the case, send an email to support@snapchat.com.

9. **Report abuse:** If a child is receiving inappropriate photos or videos, or is the victim of harassment, contact Snapchat at safety@snapchat.com.

10. **Delete the account:** If you are unhappy with Snapchat, delete the account by going to http://www.shapchat.com/a/deletion_request.pdf.

Popular instant messaging sites

- **Snapchat:** Image and short video messaging app in which the message is set to "expire" or vanish after being viewed. Users can draw on the image, add filters and text.

- **WhatsApp:** Cross-platform mobile messaging app.

- **Facebook Messenger:** Instant messaging app that allows you to send text, stickers, gifts. You're also able to create group chats and video.

- **Skype:** Instant messaging and video calls.

- **WeChat:** Mobile text and voice messaging and calling app.

- **Google Hangout:** Text, video and voice messaging and calling app. Also offers an option to share photos, emojis and chat in groups.

- **FaceTime:** Video calling app for Apple devices.

- **Viber:** Instant messaging app. You can also share video and audio messages.

- **BBM:** Instant messaging app that allows non-Blackberry users to chat with others using BBM. Offers voice calling, photos and file sharing.

- **LINE:** Instant messaging for text, images, video and audio.

- **Kik:** Platform that allows users to share photos, videos and sketches.

2. In Your Vehicle

Your family vehicle is learning more about who's behind the wheel — everything from where you like to shop to how hard you brake — as automakers roll out new tech-savvy features. Onboard navigation systems can tell where a vehicle is and where it has been. Electronic components stream data to computers that gauge driver behavior and the vehicle's roadworthiness. Vehicles recognize drivers and adjust settings for them. Infotainment systems allow voice and data communications.

"With connectivity, cars are becoming highly efficient data harvesting machines," says a 2015 study by the British Columbia Freedom of Information and Privacy Association (FIPA) on these developments.[7] Customer data generated by the connected vehicle is now seen as a major new source of revenue for marketers and advertisers, the study found. Some insurance companies are offering coverage that sets premiums based on driving patterns.

When tracked, combined, or linked with other available data, the information can reveal intensely private details of a person's life, making it vulnerable to abuse by thieves, stalkers, and others with malicious intent, the study says.

---

7   "The Connected Car: Who Is in the Driver's Seat?" BC Freedom of Information and Privacy Association (FIPA), accessed March 2016. fipa.bc.ca/wordpress/wp-content/uploads/2015/03/CC_execSum.pdf

It argues automakers have failed to comply with their obligations under privacy law when it comes to giving customers adequate information and choice about how their data is collected and used. The study recommends creation of data-protection regulations for the connected-vehicle and insurance industries, as well as involvement of privacy experts in the design stage of wired-vehicle research projects.

Vincent Gogolek, Executive Director of the BC association, believes the issue will be very important for the industry, government, and public. "There is still time to make choices and design systems that will protect privacy, but that window is closing quickly." With vehicles collecting and even sharing more personal data, Canada's privacy watchdog is quietly trying to ensure manufacturers, retailers, and insurance companies avoid bumps on the virtual highway.

The federal privacy commissioner's office, which financially supported the BC study, is "actively following" the issues and has held discussions with industry players and provincial regulators, Valerie Lawton, a spokesperson for the commissioner, told The Canadian Press (CP).[8]

The Canadian Vehicle Manufacturers Association, which represents the country's largest carmakers, initiated a meeting with the federal commissioner's office in June 2015, say notes disclosed to CP under the *Access to Information Act*. Federal privacy officials saw it as an opportunity to get a better sense of the information collected by intelligent cars, what might be coming, and whether manufacturers were fully aware of their obligations, the notes indicate.

Legal and regulatory requirements are considered whenever carmakers look at introducing new technologies with privacy implications, said Mark Nantais, Manufacturers' Association President.

"We're fully compliant — and intend to be fully compliant — with the laws that are applicable," Nantais said in an interview.

The internal notes from the privacy commissioner paint a futuristic scenario involving in-car advertising; for instance, a near-empty gas-tank sensor could project an advisory on the windshield offering the driver a discount at a nearby filling station.

Nantais, however, played down the notion wired cars produce a bounty of valuable information. "Is it myth or reality that the data actually exists?

8   "Smart Cars That Share Revealing Info about Drivers Catch Privacy Watchdog's Eye," Jim Bronskill, The Canadian Press, accessed March 2016. thecanadianpress.com/english/online/ OnlineFullStory.aspx?filename=DOR-MNN-CP.ed7b1ed59c484aa39f4c837bfb26600f.CPKE Y2008111303&newsitemid=36133067&languageid=1

That's a valid question," he said. "Some people think that everything under the sun is available, and I don't think that's the case."

A December 2013 report by the US Government Accountability Office examined the practices of ten companies (e.g., auto manufacturers, portable navigation device firms, and developers of map and navigation applications for mobile devices) that collected data to provide drivers with location-based services.

Some firms used this data to provide directions to drivers, advising them when and where to turn. Nine companies said they shared location data with others, such as traffic-information providers, in order to offer services, the report says. Two companies said they shared data stripped of personal information for other reasons, such as research, and this was "not always disclosed to consumers."

"All 10 selected companies have taken steps consistent with some, but not all, industry-recommended privacy practices," the report says. "In addition, the companies' privacy practices were, in certain instances, unclear, which could make it difficult for consumers to understand the privacy risks that may exist."[9]

The FIPA report notes that the United States lacks cross-sectoral data-protection legislation such as Canada's private-sector privacy law. "Privacy law in the US is best characterized as a patchwork of sector-specific and issue-specific laws at both federal and state levels, leaving significant geographic and subject-matter gaps."

Still, at least 15 US states have already enacted laws that give the vehicle owner control over data — concerning such things as speed, braking, and air-bag deployment — recorded by embedded devices in the event of a crash.

The state laws require that manufacturers of automobiles equipped with data recorders disclose in the owner's manual the recorder's existence along with the type of data recorded, stored, or transmitted on the device, the FIPA report says. These laws designate the car's owner as the owner of the recorder data and prohibit third-party access to the recorder without consent.

"Exceptions include release pursuant to a valid court order or search warrant, for research purposes or for diagnostic purposes such as servicing or repairing the vehicle," the FIPA report notes. In addition, some

---

9   "In-Car Location-Based Services," US Government Accountability Office gao.gov/assets/660/
    659509.pdf

states forbid insurance companies from requiring access to such data, or from penalizing customers because they refuse to allow access.

3. At the Border

In the post-9/11 era, crossing the border — once a fairly quick and pain-less process — has become more of a headache. Indeed, traveling almost anywhere in the world involves heightened scrutiny as officials demand, collect, and consult more information about people on the move.

Travelers who once breezed through the world's longest undefended border, between Canada and the United States, now face stiffer identi-fication requirements. Border-related security measures imposed by the two countries are deepening as they pursue a perimeter security pact that involves more information sharing.

Sylvie Ménard returned home to Montreal from a relaxing vacation in Mexico in 2009 to a most uncomfortable welcome: Canadian border agents made her strip to see if she had a pink tattoo on her buttocks after mixing her up with an alleged criminal.

The 43-year-old manager of a wine business had no history of trou-ble with the law. But after being questioned by an airport customs of-ficial she was pulled aside. Her luggage was tested for drug residue and her name was run through a computer. Next, a border officer read out her rights, handcuffed her, and led her to a cell.

"I was really stressed," Ménard told The Canadian Press.[10]

As far as Ménard can tell, her name matched that of a suspected criminal with the same birth date. Police were called. Ménard says it felt like a bad dream and she was astounded when a female border officer asked her to expose her backside to look for the tattoo. The officer later made her disrobe again to check if one had been erased with a laser.

Police checks turned up a different description for the suspect. Mé-nard said a police officer suggested she change her name to avoid future confusion. "That was the solution." Ménard says there must be an easier way to verify identity, given that she was carrying a passport, driver's license, and health card.

A spokesperson for the Canada Border Services Agency said he could not discuss the case, but said false matches occur and such checks

---

10 "Angry Woman Stripped at Border over Tattoo," Jim Bronskill, The Canadian Press, accessed March 2016. thestar.com/news/canada/2009/06/15/angry_woman_stripped_at_border_over_tattoo.htm

are necessary. "We can't let someone enter the country unless we're absolutely certain about [his or her] identity."

As the Canadian privacy commissioner notes, land crossings and seaports — and especially airports — are different from most other public spaces. "On the street, you would be understandably upset if police randomly demanded to examine your identification or subject you to searches."

3.1 Crossing into Canada

The commissioner's office has prepared a helpful fact sheet ("Checking In: Your Privacy Rights at Airports and Border Crossings") that we summarize here to explain more about what to expect at the border and steps to take if you feel your rights have been disrespected.[11]

What data is being collected? Under the 2011 Canada-US perimeter security initiative, the two countries agreed to set up coordinated systems to track entry and exit information from travelers. For the moment, the tracking system involves exchanging entry information collected from people at the land border so that data on place and time of entry to one country serves as a record of exit from the other.

The first two phases of the program have been limited to foreign nationals and permanent residents of Canada and the United States, but not to citizens of either country. The initiative was to be expanded by June 30, 2014, to include information-sharing on all travelers crossing the land border. In addition, Canada planned to begin collecting information on people leaving by plane, something the US already does, by requiring airlines to submit passenger manifest data for outbound international flights. Canadian officials have said work continues on the final phases, though no revised dates have been disclosed. The US has legislative authority to proceed, but Canada would need to pass a bill.

The Canada Border Services Agency plans to use the information to track the movement of suspected fugitives, child sex offenders, smugglers, and terrorists, as well as identify people who remain in Canada past visa-expiration dates and help determine when those slated for deportation have voluntarily left. The Canadian government also hopes the data will help federal agencies avoid paying hundreds of millions of dollars in social benefits now going to people who shouldn't receive them due to absences from the country.[12]

11 "Checking In: Your Privacy Rights at Airports and Border Crossings," Office of the Privacy Commissioner of Canada, accessed March 2016. priv.gc.ca/resource/fs-fi/02_05_d_45_e.asp
12 "Snowbirds Could See Fewer Social Benefits under New Security Program," Jim Bronskill, The Canadian Press, accessed March 2016. theglobeandmail.com/report-on-business/snowbirds-could-see-fewer-social-benefits-under-new-security-program/article26998777/?click=sf_globe

The Canadian border agency uses the Advance Passenger Information/Passenger Name Record (API/PNR) program to gather personal information about people arriving in Canada, including name, birth date, gender, citizenship, travel document data, itinerary, address, ticket payment information, frequent flyer information, baggage details, and contact telephone numbers. The data is checked against watch lists and databases, and individuals deemed to pose a security risk could receive additional scrutiny upon arrival. The information is stored for three-and-a-half years and may be shared with other agencies, subject to legal restrictions.

The federal border agency uses the Integrated Customs Enforcement System to collect basic information — including purpose of travel and goods purchased abroad — about people crossing the Canada-US border at major airports, some highway crossings, and cruise ship ports. Computers crunch the data to pinpoint suspicious travel patterns, which could result in extra scrutiny at the border. The system also enables border services officers to create lookout flags for specific travelers or vehicles. Personal information is kept in the system for six years.

The Canada Border Services Agency administers more than 90 acts, regulations, and international agreements — which cover everything from immigration to plants and animals — giving officers authority to conduct secondary inspections.

As the privacy commissioner notes, the courts have typically recognized that people should have reduced expectations of privacy at border points — meaning rights guaranteed by the Charter of Rights and Freedoms are limited "by factors such as sovereignty, immigration control, taxation and security."

Border officers can search through vehicles, baggage, and belongings including files, photos, and contacts on laptops and smartphones, all without a court-approved warrant. According to the border agency, an officer may do the following:[13]

- Ask you to provide detailed information about your plans while visiting the country, or the time you spent abroad.

- Make further inquiries, check records, or conduct research to verify your customs declaration.

- Confirm the guardianship of children traveling with you.

- Process the payment of duty and taxes.

---

13 "Secondary Services and Inspections," Canada Border Services Agency, accessed March 2016. cbsa-asfc.gc.ca/travel-voyage/ssi-sis-eng.html

- Conduct a visual examination of your pet or any animals traveling with you.

- Ask you to produce evidence of the money you have available to fund your visit to Canada.

- Request that you produce receipts to account for expenses you incurred or purchases made abroad.

- Count your cash or travelers' checks, in your presence.

It's possible to request a copy of your personal API/PNR data. You may ask that a notation be added to the file should any information be inaccurate (see Resources). Contact the border agency's recourse directorate to dispute any decision or search (cbsa-asfc.gc.ca/recourse-recours/menu-eng.html).

3.2 Crossing into the United States

In the United States, Customs and Border Protection and Immigration and Customs Enforcement (agencies of the Department of Homeland Security) have powers much like those of their Canadian counterparts to scrutinize travelers and goods crossing the border.

Upon entering the US, you almost certainly will be interviewed by a Customs and Border Protection agent who will collect your customs declaration. Immigration and Customs Enforcement investigates possible violations of laws and regulations.

As Homeland Security's former Chief Privacy Officer, Mary Ellen Callahan, has noted, the US Supreme Court and Congress have long held that there is no expectation of privacy for materials and goods carried over the US border, regardless of one's status in the United States.[14]

Homeland Security's Callahan recognized the sensitivity of searches of electronic devices in issuing a privacy impact assessment spelling out how such inspections should be conducted to fulfill the department's mission while respecting the rights of travelers.[15] Callahan also tried to reassure travelers by putting the issue in perspective, noting that between October 1, 2008, and August 11, 2009, Customs and Border Protection encountered more than 221 million travelers at US ports of entry.

---

14 "Privacy Issues in Border Searches of Electronic Devices," Mary Ellen Callahan, Chief Privacy Officer, US Department of Homeland Security, accessed March 2016. dhs.gov/sites/default/files/publications/privacy_privacy_issues_border_searches_electronic_devices.pdf
15 "Privacy Impact Assessment for the Border Searches of Electronic Devices," Mary Ellen Callahan, Chief Privacy Officer, US Department of Homeland Security, accessed March 2016. dhs.gov/xlibrary/assets/privacy/privacy_pia_cbp_laptop.pdf

"Approximately 1,000 laptop searches were performed in these instances — or roughly one laptop search for every 442 jumbo jets full of 500 passengers each. The vast majority of these searches were as simple as asking the traveler to power on the device to show that it is what it purports to be."

Even so, there is plenty of advice for travelers wary of crossing the border with electronic files they wish to remain private — particularly given the ubiquity of smartphones and other portable devices that hold a wealth of information. The Electronic Frontier Foundation, devoted to defending digital rights, has produced "Defending Privacy at the US Border: A Guide for Travelers Carrying Digital Devices" that offers detailed tips on shielding data.

"For doctors, lawyers, and many business professionals, these border searches can compromise the privacy of sensitive professional information, including trade secrets, attorney-client and doctor-patient communications, research and business strategies, some of which a traveler has legal and contractual obligations to protect," the guide says. "For the rest of us, searches that can reach our personal correspondence, health information, and financial records are reasonably viewed as an affront to privacy and dignity and inconsistent with the values of a free society."

One option is to travel with an alternate smartphone and laptop that contain no sensitive data and can be wiped clean upon returning home. Or you can buy a separate laptop hard drive, install a fresh operating system on it, and use it in your computer while on the road, the Foundation's guide suggests.

You can use the *US Freedom of Information Act* to see if the Homeland Security agencies have files about you. US citizens and lawful permanent residents can use the *Privacy Act*. Contact Customs and Border Protection about a concern or complaint. You can file a civil rights complaint against Customs and Border Protection or Immigration and Customs Enforcement with the Department of Homeland Security. (See Resources for links.)

If you have been repeatedly referred to secondary screening, or suspect your name is on a watch list, you may want to contact Homeland Security's Traveler Redress Inquiry Program.

4. At the Airport

Six-year-old Syed Adam Ahmed just wanted to go to a hockey game. Adam's father, Sulemaan Ahmed, tweeted a photo from Toronto's international airport that appeared to show the boy's name with a "DHP" or "deemed high profile" label and instructions on how to proceed before allowing the youngster to check in. They were trying to board an Air Canada flight December 31, 2015, to Boston to see the NHL Winter Classic.[16]

Tales of other children with the same sorts of travel challenges soon emerged. Adam's mother, Cajee, has become an unofficial liaison with the Liberal government on behalf of many families.

"When they saw this in the media, they contacted us," said Cajee. "Because I guess they were surprised and happy to know they were not the only ones."

It's still unclear what's going on, but Public Safety Minister Ralph Goodale promised to look at the Canadian no-fly regime, known as the Passenger Protect Program, as part of a broader national-security review. Under the program, the public safety minister establishes a list of people about whom there are reasonable grounds to suspect they will:

- engage or attempt to engage in an act that would threaten transportation security; or

- travel by air to commit certain terrorism offenses, such as participating in or contributing to terrorist activities.

The minister must review these listing decisions at least every 90 days. The criteria for inclusion on the list were recently broadened beyond those who simply posed an "immediate threat" to aviation security.

The name, birth date, and gender of each listed person are provided to airlines so they can check the information against those taking flights originating from, destined for, or flying within Canada.

Air carriers must cross-reference the list with all passengers who appear to be 18 years of age or older before issuing them a boarding pass.[17] If there is a match, the airline must confirm the person's identity and inform Transport Canada.

---

16 "Dozens of Families with No-fly List Hassles Contact Ontario Boy's Mother," Jim Bronskill, The Canadian Press, accessed March 2016. citynews.ca/2016/01/20/dozens-of-families-with-no-fly-list-hassles-contact-ontario-boys-mother

17 "How the Passenger Protect Program Works," Public Safety Canada, accessed March 2016. publicsafety.gc.ca/cnt/ntnl-scrt/cntr-trrrsm/pssngr-prtct/hw-pssngr-prtct-wrks-eng.aspx

In the event of a positive match, the public safety minister may then direct the airline to take action to prevent the individual from carrying out the prohibited activities outlined above. It might mean telling the carrier to forbid the person from boarding a plane or demanding that he or she undergo additional screening.

If you are denied boarding due to presence on the Canadian no-fly list, you will be given written notice confirming so. You then have 60 days to challenge the decision to the Passenger Protect Recourse Office.

Only one person is publicly known to have been prevented from boarding a plane due to being on the Canadian no-fly list. Hani Al Telbani of Longueuil, Quebec, was denied a seat on an Air Canada flight from Montreal to Riyadh, Saudi Arabia, via London, on June 4, 2008. Within days, the master's student in information system security at Concordia University applied to the federal Office of Reconsideration (the appeal body at the time) and filed suit in the Federal Court, alleging the no-fly program breached guarantees under the Charter of Rights and Freedoms. A 2008 report commissioned by the appeal office said Telbani should never have been barred from the flight.

Canada followed the lead of the United States in establishing the list in 2007. The American no-fly roster — believed to be much larger than the Canadian one — has been heavily criticized by civil libertarians.

Ottawa insisted a Canadian version was necessary to guard against terrorists and others out to cause serious trouble aboard aircraft. Critics called it a violation of human rights with no guarantee of increased safety.

In announcing his review of the program, Goodale reminded airlines there is no need to check people younger than 18 against the no-fly list.

Complicating matters is the fact Air Canada, the country's largest airline, is known to use US aviation security lists, though it refuses to discuss the practice. This could account for many of the hassles Canadians, including youngsters, experience at the airport.

We do know that the US Transportation Security Administration's Secure Flight program allows for collection of the name, gender, and birth date of the some five million Canadians who cross American airspace each year en route to destinations such as the Caribbean, Mexico, and South America — even if their planes don't touch American soil. The US agency runs the names against security lists.

Secure Flight uses this basic biographic data about travelers to try to identify both low-risk and high-risk passengers before they arrive at the airport through cross-referencing. The program then issues screening instructions to airlines, categorizing passengers —

- who are eligible for expedited screening,

- who will receive standard screening,

- on the Selectee List and therefore designated for enhanced screening, and

- on the US No-Fly List or Centers for Disease Control and Prevention Do Not Board List, and therefore ineligible to fly. (The No-Fly List is a subset of a database maintained by the Federal Bureau of Investigation's Terrorist Screening Center.)

Travelers, including non-Americans, who experience screening-related or inspection difficulties can pursue a remedy through the Department of Homeland Security's Traveler Redress Inquiry Program.

Moreover, in March 2016, Canada and the US agreed to set up a Redress Working Group to help resolve errors of identity on no-fly lists. In a statement, Canada said the new processes would help expedite processing of complaints and streamline security-list removal procedures. In addition, Canada and the US will routinely share their respective no-fly lists as part of a joint effort to identify threats.

Air travelers worldwide have become used to the pre-boarding ritual of placing items in trays, lifting one's arms, and even removing footwear for security screeners.

The US Transportation Security Administration and Canadian Air Transport Security Authority have generally similar screening procedures involving walk-through metal detectors, physical searches, full-body scanners, and explosive-trace detection.

You might undergo additional screening due to random selection because you tripped a detector alarm, or the fact you must avoid the detector because of a pacemaker or other such device.

In addition to a visual search under accessories such as scarves, the screening officer may also carry out a "pat down" to check for concealed objects. You can ask that a pat down take place in a private area and that an officer of the same gender wears gloves during the procedure. A second officer is also supposed to be present.

In airports equipped with millimeter-wave full-body scanners, you may choose this option or a physical search if required to undergo additional screening. However, in a small number of cases US screeners will require a full-body scan. The scanners, which detect weapons and explosives not caught by metal detectors, generate a stick-figure image of the passenger rather than a detailed outline. It can alert screeners to an area of the body requiring additional search.

If your checked baggage is opened and inspected, a notice to that effect will be placed inside.

The United States and Canada have also embraced similar advanced data-crunching techniques to try to pinpoint potentially dangerous travelers. The Canada Border Services Agency has ushered in scenario-based targeting (already used by the US) as part of Canada's commitment to cooperate with Washington under the 2011 continental security pact known as the Beyond the Border initiative.

Commercial airlines are legally bound to provide Canada's border agency with specific information about passengers flying to Canada, including name, birth date, citizenship, seat number, and other details. The border agency has long used the information to assess people for risk, allowing officials to zero in on those with high scores for additional attention upon landing. The new scenario-based scheme uses elaborate number-crunching, or Big Data analytics, to reveal patterns in the information provided by air carriers — a method the border agency considers more efficient and accurate.

Privacy Commissioner Daniel Therrien is pressing the border agency to explain the program's rationale and build in safeguards to protect individual liberties. Travelers may be targeted if they fit the general attributes of a group due to traits they cannot change such as age, gender, nationality, birthplace, and racial or ethnic origin, he warns.

In his recently released annual report, Therrien said, "it could allow the operator to, for example, search for all males aged between the ages of 18–20 who are Egyptian nationals and who have visited both Paris and New York."[18]

The border agency says scenarios are "a generic set of indicators" that flow from analysis of intelligence, enforcement, trends, and other

---

18 "Thousands Flying to Canada Flagged for Security Checks by New System," Jim Bronskill, The Canadian Press, accessed March 2016. thestar.com/news/canada/2016/01/14/thousands-flying-to-canada-flagged-for-security-checks-by-new-system.html

information to identify passengers who "may pose a higher risk" due to concerns about national security, smuggling of contraband such as drugs, or illicit migration. This could mean additional scrutiny for some travelers when their plane touches down in Canada.

You can take action by doing the following (links are provided in the Resources at the end of this book):

- Contact the Department of Homeland Security Traveler Redress Inquiry Program.

- File a complaint with the US Transportation Security Administration (TSA).

- Make an application to the Passenger Protect Recourse Office (Public Safety Canada).

- File a complaint with the Canadian Air Transport Security Authority (CATSA).

- File a complaint regarding damage or lost items because of a CATSA search.

5. Staying Secure On the Move

Phones, tablets, and laptops are popular targets for both physical and data theft, warns Public Safety Canada,[19] the counterpart of US Homeland Security. "These devices offer a centralized source of information, both personal and professional, about you and the organization for which you work or represent."

Here are some useful tips from Public Safety on avoiding cyber-theft on the road.

Before you go:

- Protect all your devices with strong passwords or passcodes. Do not use the same code on more than one device. (See the earlier section on Passwords in Chapter 4.)

- Minimize the data contained on your device. Only include information that you will need for your travel.

- To avoid losing valuable information, back up all important files and store them in a separate location.

---

19 http://www.getcybersafe.gc.ca/cnt/prtct-yrslf/prtct-trvl/index-en.aspx

- Some devices have an option that will erase all data if the password is repeatedly entered incorrectly. Enable this option so that if you lose the device, that's all you'll lose.

- Update any software and security patches.

- Do some research on the laws and regulations of the country you plan to visit, as you are subject to the laws governing intellectual property, digital information, censorship, and encrypted data in that country. As we have discussed, sensitive business information on your devices may be subject to search at border crossings.

While abroad:

- Do not let your devices out of your sight.

- Avoid charging your phone or device by plugging it into a computer or other device that you do not control. Malicious software could be transferred when your device is connected. Plug directly into a wall socket instead.

- Turn your Bluetooth off when you're not using it. Some devices allow for automatic connection, meaning other Bluetooth networks can connect to your device without authorization.

- Turn off your devices completely when not in use. Don't allow them to be in "sleep" mode.

- Be aware that Wi-Fi hotspots are common targets for identity thieves. These networks may be unsecure and accessible to anyone. Unless you are using a secure Web page, you should never send or receive private information when using public Wi-Fi. When available, use a hard-wired connection.

- If you plan on using Wi-Fi provided by your hotel, ask what security measures are taken to protect the guests' information.

- Free Internet access points are sometimes established for malicious or deceitful purposes. These Internet access points are purposely named to imitate trusted access points. For example, a hotel may have established an access point called HotelABC Internet. A malicious individual may set up a misleading or deceptive access point in the vicinity of that hotel called SecureHotelABC Internet. This access point may even have better signal strength than the legitimate one. You should confirm with your hotel the name of any Internet connection it provides.

- Be careful about broadcasting your travel plans. For example, avoid posting updates and photos that reveal your whereabouts on social media sites.

On your return home:

- Reset credentials for access to your device and all accounts, including personal accounts (even if not accessed while abroad) that have similar usernames and/or passwords. These may include banking, social networking and webmail accounts.

If you are traveling outside North America on government or corporate business, there are special precautions you should consider. Canada's main spy agency, the Canadian Security Intelligence Service, produced a guide for senior personnel warning of the dangers from state agents out to pilfer confidential files.

A copy of the 2012 CSIS publication, *Far from home: A travel security guide for government officials*, was obtained by The Canadian Press under the Access to Information Act.

Among the spy service's advice:

- Information you provide on a visa application form could be used to assess your worthiness as a target, meaning only necessary details should be provided. For example, some countries will request passport numbers of family members, even if they are not traveling with you.

- Travel with an alternate telecommunications device that contains no sensitive data and can be wiped clean when you return home. You do not want to take abroad a device packed with emails, contacts and documents.

- Conceal baggage tags and assume luggage will be searched in transit.

- Any details given to airline or border control agents may be collected by the host country — or shared with other countries.

- Border searches may entail copying of documents, including those on a laptop or smartphone.

- Classified documents are best kept on one's person or in secure storage at your country's embassy.

- While some might think foreign spies are after only big-ticket quarry like fighter jet plans, they might simply covet a government agency's personnel organization chart.

- Know that in many countries you will be subject to physical surveillance.

- Never talk shop or volunteer information in front of taxi drivers, waiters and bartenders, who could be intelligence officers or informants. Every little bit of information can be useful to a competitor.

- Be wary of gifts such as digital memory keys that can give someone remote access to a computer once plugged in.

- Foreign agents may employ the relatively subtle technique of eliciting information through random conversation, perhaps appealing to one's ego or emphasizing mutual interests.

- Some travelers have returned to their hotel rooms to find people searching their belongings or conducting unnecessary maintenance activities. Intrusions are frequently accomplished with the co-operation of hotel staff.

- Beware the "honey trap" — sexual seduction as a means of blackmail through the secret recording of an intimate encounter. There are also reports of individuals who have suspected they were drugged and who awoke to find that their hotel room had been searched, smartphone stolen and secret business documents missing.

- In some countries the threat of kidnapping is significant, as many groups depend on such activities to fund their operations. Consequently, you may want to look for signs of hostile reconnaissance, as well as to vary your routines and the routes you take to and from your hotel and place of work.

6

Pictures and Videos in Public Spaces

The digital age has drastically changed the way we take and share photographs and videos. Today, anyone, anywhere, can use smartphones to photograph and take videos in public spaces — as opposed to inside a home, vehicle, or any other personal and intimate space. These photos and videos can be shared instantly on various social media sites.

In light of what we've learned so far in this book, the following questions may spring to mind:

- What rights do you have as a photographer?

- Are you free to distribute photos and videos on the Internet?

- Are you allowed to take a photograph anywhere, of anyone?

- What restrictions are there on photographs taken of you?

- What rights to do you have to refuse, or to stipulate that the photos not be circulated?

This chapter is not meant to be a definitive guide on the dos and don'ts of taking photos and videos in public places. Nor does it constitute legal advice. Rather, it poses three basic questions to keep in mind.

I. Do I Need the Person's Permission?

In Canada you do not generally need permission to photograph or take a video of a person for the purposes of personal photography. However, for activities considered to be commercial, privacy protections usually require consent.

Privacy protections set out in the federal *Personal Information Protection and Electronic Documents Act* (PIPEDA) apply to personal information collected in the course of commercial activities. In most cases, PIPEDA requires a photographer to obtain consent from an individual who will be identifiable in a photograph. This requirement does not apply to photographs taken solely for journalistic, artistic, or literary purposes.

You do not need permission if you're taking public crowd photos that do not focus on anyone in particular, but on the crowd more generally.

In the United States the rules are much looser. There is no distinction between commercial and noncommercial use.

"The United States has always been among the most, absolutist (countries) on free speech," says Jay Stanley, Senior Policy Analyst with the American Civil Liberties Union's Speech, Privacy and Technology Project. "When you are in public, and you're in a place where you have a right to be, you have a right to take photographs of anything that is in plain view. Our courts have found that that is a First Amendment right, a free speech right. Photography is a form of art. It can be a very important means of allowing the citizenry to monitor its government. And the rights of photographers have been mostly upheld."

2. What Rights Do I Have to Not be Photographed?

In Canada, you have no right to control the use of your image if it's taken for private photographic purposes, but you do have rights if the picture is taken for commercial purposes, says David Fewer, Director of the Canadian Internet Policy and Public Interest Clinic (CIPPIC).

In the United States, you have little control over how and when a photograph or video is taken of you in public, or how it is used.

"It is a difficult issue," says Jay Stanley. "Because just as you have a First Amendment right to curse at somebody, it's not necessarily acceptable behavior. It can be very impolite and it makes people angry.

And I think taking photographs of people when they don't want you to is similar in that respect. So part of why people react badly is because in polite company, you don't stick a camera in someone's face if [he or she doesn't] want it."

You have the right to be free from harassment, or being stalked if you've asked the person to stop. Someone taking your photograph does not have the right to interfere with you, for instance, by blocking a public road or sidewalk, or preventing you from entering your personal property.

Note that you cannot threaten to destroy the individual's camera, lens, film, or any other public property. Nor can you search the individual's bags, vehicle, or other possessions.

3. Where Can I Take the Photo or Shoot the Video?

You can take photos on public property, such as sidewalks. This includes taking photos of anything that a normal person could see from a location in a public space.

You can take photos on another person's property, where you have permission from the owner, property manager, security guard, or other representative of the owner.

You can also take photos on property that is privately owned, but open to the public, such as malls and galleries. However, it is both wise and polite to ask permission.

7

Spying Eyes

The dispute between the US Federal Bureau of Investigation and Apple (discussed in Chapter 4) over law-enforcement access to a customer's data is emblematic of a recurring question in the digital age: Do new technologies provide criminals with the unprecedented ability to "go dark" or effectively hide evidence of their misdeeds from authorities?

Police are genuinely concerned that everyone from money launderers to child pornographers will be allowed to commit their heinous crimes with impunity if officers of the law are barred from patrolling

some stretches of cyberspace. At the same time, civil libertarians and privacy advocates say such concerns do not warrant trampling the freedom of law-abiding people to communicate without fear of state intrusion.

In the following sections we look at privacy rights when dealing with police and intelligence services in both the virtual and physical realms.

Surveillance

1. Surveillance is expanding rapidly — our newly digital existence has dramatically multiplied possibilities for surveillance.

2. The accelerating demand for greater security drives much surveillance.

3. Public and private agencies are increasingly intertwined.

4. It is more difficult to decide what information is private and what is not.

5. Mobile and location-based surveillance is expanding.

6. Surveillance practices and processes are becoming globalized.

7. Surveillance is now embedded in everyday environments such as vehicles, buildings, and homes.

8. The human body is increasingly a source of surveillance. Fingerprinting, iris scanning, facial recognition, and DNA records are now commonly used to identify individuals.

9. Social surveillance is growing — social media has facilitated an explosion of digitally enabled people watching.

(Source: *Transparent Lives: Surveillance in Canada,* Athabasca University Press)

I. Police

We have all seen terrible images in the news that depict the wrenching aftermath of a police shooting — a most disturbing event that leaves a family grieving, a community in shock, and an officer traumatized.

However, most encounters with police are routine: Words exchanged at a protest, some questions after a traffic stop, or perhaps a doorstep discussion with an investigator. Still, such interactions can cause anxiety and make us wonder what we are obligated to do under the law.

The American Civil Liberties Union (ACLU) has prepared a guide with tips should you be stopped in the US by police, immigration agents, or the Federal Bureau of Investigation.[1]

Your rights:

- You have the right to remain silent. If you wish to exercise that right, say so out loud.

- You have the right to refuse to consent to a search of yourself, your vehicle, or your home.

- If you are not under arrest, you have the right to calmly leave.

- You have the right to a lawyer if you are arrested. Ask for one immediately.

- Regardless of your immigration or citizenship status, you have constitutional rights.

Your responsibilities:

- Do stay calm and be polite.

- Do not interfere with or obstruct the police.

- Do not lie or give false documents.

- Do prepare yourself and your family in case you are arrested.

- Do remember the details of the encounter.

- Do file a written complaint or call your local ACLU if you feel your rights have been violated.

---

1   "Know Your Rights: What to Do If You're Stopped by Police, Immigration Agents or the FBI," American Civil Liberties Union (ACLU), accessed March 2016. aclu.org/know-your-rights/what-do-if-youre-stopped-police-immigration-agents-or-fbi

The Canadian Civil Liberties Association (CCLA) has produced a similar basic guide spelling out your rights when dealing with the police. It says police officers can stop you under three general circumstances:[2]

- If they suspect that you have committed a crime.

- If they see you committing a crime.

- If you are driving.

If the police do not arrest you, or lack grounds to detain you, they must let you be on your way, the guide notes. It also explains your rights when stopped while driving, upon being arrested, and when police visit your home, and includes information on how and where to make complaints.

Traditionally, warrants granted by independent judges have been the primary tool for ensuring that police search powers are used appropriately and reasonably, the CCLA says.

"However, this balance is constantly being challenged by changes in the law and technology. Certain searches — like wiretaps, strip searches and DNA collection — are so invasive that additional protections are necessary, and rapid technological changes are profoundly expanding the amount of information captured about our daily lives."[3]

Constant vigilance is needed to ensure a reasonable balance, and that privacy protections remain both meaningful and effective, the association says.

The organization's in-depth examination of police record checks revealed that forces were disclosing information to prospective employers and others, including records of suicide attempts, complaints where charges were never laid, and withdrawn charges and acquittals.

People with non-conviction records are being excluded from school and denied jobs on the basis of unproven allegations or 911 calls they have made.

"Regular disclosure of this information prejudices the presumption of innocence, constitutes a violation of privacy, and can lead to discriminatory decisions," the CCLA says. "We believe that the time has come for Canadian organizations and governments to seriously address this issue."

2   "Know Your Rights: A Citizen's Guide to Rights When Dealing with Police," Canadian Civil Liberties Association (CCLA), accessed March 2016. ccla.org/cclanewsite/wp-content/uploads/2015/02/Know-Your-Rights-Booklet.pdf

3   "Policing and Public Safety: Privacy, Search and Seizure, Warrants," Canadian Civil Liberties Association (CCLA), accessed March 2016. ccla.org/issues/policing-and-public-safety/privacy-search-and-seizure-warrants

Some information in the Royal Canadian Mounted Police (RCMP) databases, while legitimately gathered during criminal investigations, was either kept longer than needed or retained when it should have been purged, the federal privacy commissioner found in a study.[4]

If you feel your rights have been violated, you may want to take the issue up directly with the relevant police force or contact the following agencies:

- American Civil Liberties Union

- US Department of Justice Office of the Inspector General

- Canadian Civil Liberties Association

- Civilian Review and Complaints Commission for the RCMP

- Canadian Association of Police Governance

2. Intelligence Agencies

The Canadian inquiry into the Maher Arar affair opened many eyes to a hidden world. It detailed how US officials sent Arar, an Ottawa telecommunications engineer, to Syria, where he was tortured in a grim chamber and made false confessions about al-Qaida ties.

The Royal Canadian Mounted Police (RCMP), scrambling to manage the post-9/11 antiterrorism file, had given the Americans seriously flawed information about Arar, very likely prompting his year-long nightmare. The episode drove home a chilling truth: The actions of an overzealous or misguided security agency can place an innocent person in grave danger.

The Arar inquiry, led by Justice Dennis O'Connor, almost a decade ago recommended that the security activities of the Canada Border Services Agency and other organizations lacking watchdogs be subject to review. O'Connor also advocated changes to the law to allow national security watchdogs to exchange information and conduct joint investigations, as well as the creation of a coordinating committee of security watchdog chairs to ensure smooth handling of complaints and probes.

The Arar inquiry also documented not only the close relationship between major security players — both at home and abroad — but the

---

4 "Audit Report of the Privacy Commissioner of Canada: Audit of Selected RCMP Operational Databases," Office of the Privacy Commissioner of Canada, accessed March 2016. priv.gc.ca/information/pub/ar-vr/ar-vr_rcmp_2011_e.asp

spread of intelligence functions to agencies such as the immigration and transport departments.

The US intelligence community dwarfs that of Canada. In 2010, *The Washington Post* reported that some 1,271 government organizations and 1,931 private companies were working on counterterrorism, homeland security, and intelligence in about 10,000 locations across the United States.[5]

Constitutional provisions, privacy laws, and other statutes limit the actions of intelligence agencies, which rely on various authorities and tools (from judicial warrants to executive orders) to collect, use, and share information. However, there is growing concern among privacy advocates and civil libertarians that government surveillance has mushroomed out of control in the name of fighting terrorism.

The decisions intelligence agencies take may see you wind up on a watch list, face immigration or travel problems, or lose your job.

"Increasingly, the government is engaged in suspicion-less surveillance that vacuums up and tracks sensitive information about innocent people," says the American Civil Liberties Union (ACLU). "The erosion of reasonable restrictions on government's power to collect people's personal information is putting the privacy and free speech rights of all Americans at risk."

Says Gus Hosein, London-based director of Privacy International, "For over a decade we all fought a sham democratic debate over the powers that were acceptable in a democratic society, and in secret they just took on new powers."[6]

We could easily devote the entire book to describing the security intelligence realm and the privacy implications posed by the activities of the alphabet soup of agencies that operate in the shadows. However, let's take a look at a handful of key recent developments with implications for privacy.

The previous Conservative government in Ottawa enacted the most significant changes to security laws in more than a decade. The controversial bill, known as C-51, gave the Canadian Security Intelligence Service (CSIS) more power to thwart suspected terrorist plots by, for

---

5   "A Hidden World, Growing Beyond Control," Dana Priest and William M. Arkin, *The Washington Post*, accessed March 2016. projects.washingtonpost.com/top-secret-america/articles/a-hidden-world-growing-beyond-control
6   "Spy Files: ACLU Campaign to Expose and Stop Illegal Domestic Spying," American Civil Liberties Union (ACLU), accessed March 2016. aclu.org/feature/spy-files

instance, canceling airline reservations or meddling with computers — going well beyond its long-standing information-gathering role. CSIS would need a warrant in order to carry out disruption activities that breach the Charter of Rights and Freedoms. Critics say this amounts to an extraordinary inversion of the judiciary's role.

The legislation also creates a new offense of promoting the commission of terrorist offenses and broadens the government's no-fly list powers. In addition, it greatly expands the sharing of federally held information about activity that "undermines the security of Canada." The law faces a constitutional challenge, but the new Liberal government has promised to repeal "problematic elements" of the bill as part of a major revamp of the national-security apparatus. Canadians will get a chance to have their say as to whether the Conservatives went too far.

The review might well delve into the RCMP's desire for warrantless access to Internet subscriber information to keep pace with extremists, child predators, and other online criminals.[7]

In June 2014, the Supreme Court of Canada ruled police need judicial authorization to obtain subscriber data linked to online activities. The high court rejected the notion the federal privacy law governing companies allowed them to hand over subscriber identities voluntarily. Police say telecommunications companies and other service providers (e.g., banks and rental companies) now demand court approval for nearly all types of requests from authorities for basic identifying information.

RCMP Commissioner Bob Paulson advocates an administrative scheme that would give police ready access to a telecommunications customer's name and address while respecting the Charter of Rights and Freedoms. However, it is not clear how that would work.

Documents leaked in 2013 by former American spy contractor Edward Snowden revealed the US National Security Agency (NSA) had quietly obtained access to a huge volume of electronic mail, chat logs, and other information from major Internet companies, as well as massive amounts of data about telephone calls. As a result, privacy advocates and opposition politicians demanded assurances the NSA's Canadian counterpart, the Communications Security Establishment (CSE), was not using its extraordinary powers to snoop on Canadians.

---

7   "RCMP Need Warrantless Access to Online Subscriber Info: Paulson," Jim Bronskill, The Canadian Press, accessed March 2016. cbc.ca/news/politics/paulson-rcmp-subscriber-info-warrantless-access-1.3337028

The watchdog over the CSE recently reported the spy agency broke privacy laws by sharing information about Canadians with foreign partners. The CSE passed along the information (known as metadata) to counterparts in the United States, Britain, Australia, and New Zealand. Metadata is information associated with a communication (i.e., telephone number or email address), but not the message itself. However, privacy advocates point out it can be highly revealing.

"While secrecy may be an inherent aspect of many intelligence activities, so is accountability," said a 2014 report from the Canadian privacy commissioner. "National security claims do not reduce accountability obligations and security bodies must account to Canadians for what they do with personal information."[8]

The ACLU expresses concern about several US trends, including the following:

- The Federal Bureau of Investigation's domestic intelligence work, "where its actions are largely hidden from public view and the procedural checks and balances that apply in criminal investigations are all but non-existent."[9]

- Prevalence of fusion centers (multi-jurisdictional intelligence hubs) that lack clear guidelines and proper oversight, producing information of dubious value.

- Rise of suspicious-activity reporting programs to encourage police, security officials, and the public to report allegedly unusual behavior such as using binoculars or taking pictures — potentially ensnaring innocent people.

The civil liberties union maintains this surveillance often takes place in secret, with little or no oversight by the courts, legislatures, or the public.

Indeed, asserting your privacy rights in the security intelligence realm poses challenges because of the following:

- You might never know you were spied on.

- If you do have some evidence of being surveilled, it could be difficult to know which agency or country did so.

---

8   "Checks and Controls: Reinforcing Privacy Protection and Oversight for the Canadian Intelligence Community in an Era of Cyber-Surveillance," Office of the Privacy Commissioner of Canada, accessed March 2016. priv.gc.ca/information/sr-rs/201314/sr_cic_e.asp
9   "Spy Files: The ACLU Campaign to Expose & Stope Illegal Domestic Spying," American Civil Liberties Union and the ACLU Foundation, accessed March 2016. candidcupcakes.wordpress.com/tag/fbi

- Filing a privacy-law request to the suspected agencies likely will turn up little since, if you were a target, it would not be in their operational interests to confirm interest.

Still, there are established avenues of recourse for those with complaints. Please see the Resources section of the book for details.

3. Video Surveillance

They may have had good intentions, but the operators of an unusual website (Insecam.cc) got little praise for a highly public stunt. In 2014, the site pulled together live video footage from Internet-connected cameras around the world operating with the manufacturer's default username and password.[10] It meant anyone could see the streams from tens of thousands of such cameras in homes, offices, and even daycares.

The exercise's goal was to educate people about the need to alter camera settings to ensure privacy. However, the episode prompted privacy commissioners from several countries, including Canada, Britain, and China, to threaten "enforcement action" due to the harm that could result from making the video feeds easily accessible to prying eyes.[11] It also alerted many to the hidden dangers to privacy posed by the tiny cameras.

We don't have the option to flick the off switches on the plethora of video cameras that monitor public spaces — from airports and border crossings to fairgrounds and parks. The Canadian privacy commissioner has long expressed concern about the use of cameras by police and other enforcement agencies.

"Video surveillance of public places subjects everyone to scrutiny, regardless of whether they have done anything to arouse suspicion," the commissioner's office said in 2006. "At the very least it circumscribes, if it does not eradicate outright, the expectation of privacy and anonymity that we have as we go about our daily business."[12]

The privacy commissioner issued detailed guidelines for police that stress use of video surveillance in public places should —

---

10 "Website Live Streaming Unsecured Webcams," Ryan Van Velzer, *The Arizona Republic*, accessed March 2016. usatoday.com/story/news/nation/2014/11/19/live-stream-unsecured-webcams/19289821
11 "Letter to Operators of Webcam Website," Office of the Privacy Commissioner of Canada, accessed March 2016. priv.gc.ca/media/nr-c/2014/let_141121_e.asp
12 "Guidelines for the Use of Video Surveillance of Public Places by Police and Law Enforcement Authorities," Office of the Privacy Commissioner of Canada, accessed March 2016. priv.gc.ca/information/guide/vs_060301_e.asp

- only be deployed to address a real, pressing, and substantial problem;

- be viewed as an exceptional step, only to be taken in the absence of a less privacy-invasive alternative;

- not be undertaken before the impact on privacy is assessed; and

- include public notice of the camera system.

Use of video surveillance has become particularly commonplace in Britain. It is also becoming an increasingly widespread feature of American life, notes the American Civil Liberties Union (ACLU).

"Although surveillance cameras have been around for decades, in just the last few years we have seen something entirely new in the American experience: the construction of centralized, government-run camera systems," the organization says. "The ACLU does not oppose placing cameras at specific, high-profile public places that are potential terrorist targets, such as the US Capitol. But the impulse to blanket our public spaces and streets with video surveillance is a bad idea. The growing presence of cameras will create chilling effects that bring subtle but profound changes to the character of our public spaces."[13]

---

13 "Video Surveillance," American Civil Liberties Union (ACLU), accessed March 2016. aclu.org/issues/privacy-technology/surveillance-technologies/video-surveillance

The civil liberties union sees public benefit in the trend toward police wearing small video cameras that clip on their uniforms — or may be embedded in glasses or helmets — allowing their encounters with the public to be recorded, thereby promoting accountability.

"Overall, we think they can be a win-win — but *only* if they are deployed within a framework of strong policies to ensure they protect the public without becoming yet another system for routine surveillance *of* the public," the organization says.[14]

A key question is whether such cameras should always be on or operated at the officer's discretion. Continuous recording would result in many bystanders being routinely recorded. Yet giving police authority to decide when the camera should be on might defeat the overall purpose of capturing a record of interactions.

The high-resolution digital images the new body-worn cameras produce allow for a clear view of individuals and are suited to running video analytics software, such as facial recognition, noted privacy commissioners from across Canada in a guidance document developed in 2015.

"Microphones may be sensitive enough to capture not only the sounds associated with the situation being targeted but also ambient sound that could include the conversations of bystanders."[15]

4. Drones

Drones (unmanned aerial vehicles, to be more formal) have vast potential for everything from filming movie scenes and digital mapping to wildlife management and industrial espionage. They're also used for military and police duties.

Regulators and privacy advocates are scrambling to ensure the rapidly evolving technology doesn't become an invasive headache.

Drones are often outfitted with cameras but can also carry gizmos such as thermal-imaging devices and license plate readers, noted a 2013 study for the Canadian privacy commissioner.

---

14 "Police Body-Mounted Cameras: With Right Policies in Place, a Win for All," American Civil Liberties Union (ACLU), accessed March 2016. aclu.org/police-body-mounted-cameras-right-policies-place-win-all
15 "Guidance for the Use of Body-worn Cameras by Law Enforcement Authorities," Office of the Privacy Commissioner of Canada, accessed March 2016. priv.gc.ca/information/pub/gd_bwc_201502_e.asp

The Royal Canadian Mounted Police (RCMP) has begun experimenting with small, helicopter-like drones that fit in the trunk of a car for chores such as photographing accident scenes. But the devices come even smaller. Biomimetic drones are made to resemble plants, animals, or birds. Portable ones are becoming easier to buy.

"Drones are already being sold in many retail stores," the study notes. "The next generation of recreational drones could prove to be even smaller and cheaper than the ones that currently exist."[16]

The following technologies can be mounted on drones:

- High-powered zoom lenses.

- Night-vision, infrared, and detail-enhancing capabilities.

- Radar that can track people inside buildings or through clouds or dense foliage.

- Video software that can recognize specific people, events, or objects and flag movements or changes in routine as suspicious.

- Distributed video, where several drones work in sync with multiple video cameras.

"Some of these technologies have the ability to capture data from great distances and through walls, and with a fine level of detail, for example the ability to capture the image of a person's face from miles away."

The study concludes that drone operations involving surveillance of people would be covered by "the same privacy law requirements" as any other data collection practice. However, it says organizations using drones will be expected to "genuinely address" the privacy implications of their use and ensure compliance with laws and guidelines.

"Furthermore, the advent of the smartphone has made model aircraft, and other such tools for surveillance, data, or image capture, a plausible option for recreational use by the public," the study says. "The collection or use of personal information via model aircraft for personal purposes may reach beyond the scope of privacy law."

In 2016, the Canadian government plans to introduce regulatory requirements for small drones weighing 25 kilograms or less that are operated within visual line of sight.

---

16 "Drones in Canada: Will the Proliferation of Domestic Drone Use in Canada Raise New Concerns for Privacy?" Office of the Privacy Commissioner of Canada, accessed March 2016. priv. gc.ca/information/research-recherche/2013/drones_201303_e.asp

The federal government should consider restricting the use of small camera-equipped drones in "sensitive and protected" areas such as residential neighborhoods, schoolyards, and prisons, says the federal privacy commissioner. The commissioner's office also advocates some means of identifying the operator of a drone, possibly through a license plate, painted number, or electronic signal to help the complaint process when problems arise.

In the United States, legal issues related to individuals' privacy interests protected under the Fourth Amendment have slowed the adoption of drones for domestic surveillance and homeland security operations, the Congressional Research Service recently noted.[17]

As the technology quickly evolves, the US, like Canada, faces "significant challenges" in balancing safety requirements, economic interests, and privacy concerns, the study says.

In early 2015, US President Barack Obama directed federal agencies that use drones to look at the privacy impact of the flying devices and develop policies to address concerns. As with many other issues involving personal information, however, individual states have moved to fill the void, with at least 20 bringing in drone-related laws, another Congressional Research Service primer noted.[18]

The author concluded that understanding American privacy rights with relation to drones was not as simple as applying Supreme Court case law or federal and state statutes. "Rather, regulations may come from myriad sources, some statutory, some regulatory, and some practical."

Even so, the American Civil Liberties Union has expressed concern about US law enforcement's expanded use of drones. It recommends the following safeguards:[19]

- **Usage limits:** A drone should be deployed by law enforcement only with a warrant, in an emergency, or when there are specific grounds to believe it will collect evidence relating to a criminal act.

- **Data retention:** Images should be retained only when there is reasonable suspicion that they contain evidence of a crime or are relevant to an ongoing investigation or trial.

17 "Unmanned Aircraft Operations in Domestic Airspace: US Policy Perspectives and the Regulatory Landscape," Bart Elias, Congressional Research Service, accessed March 2016. fas.org/sgp/crs/misc/R44352.pdf
18 "Domestic Drones and Privacy: A Primer," Richard M. Thompson II, Congressional Research Service, accessed March 2016. fas.org/sgp/crs/misc/R43965.pdf
19 "Domestic Drones," American Civil Liberties Union and the ACLU Foundation, accessed March 2016. aclu.org/issues/privacy-technology/surveillance-technologies/domestic-drones

- **Policy:** Usage policy on drones should be decided by the public's representatives, not by police departments, and the policies should be clear, written, and open to the public.

- **Abuse prevention and accountability:** Use of domestic drones should be subject to open audits and proper oversight to prevent misuse.

- **Weapons:** Domestic drones should not be equipped with any kind of weapon.

8

Information Requests and Complaints

Federal government agencies in the United States and Canada gather a wide array of information about people to provide essential services and to carry out their responsibilities — from issuing pension checks to enforcing laws.

However, you have the right — with some limited exceptions — to ensure the material is up-to-date and not used for unintended reasons. So how do you obtain that information?

I. Accessing Your Information in the United States

In the United States, the *Privacy Act* of 1974 dictates how federal agencies collect, maintain, use, and disseminate personal information.[1] The law guarantees the right:

- to see records about oneself;

- to request the amendment of records that are not accurate, relevant, timely or complete; and

- of individuals to be protected against unwarranted invasion of their privacy resulting from the collection, maintenance, use, and disclosure of personal information.

---

1   *Privacy Act*, US Department of State, accessed March 2016. foia.state.gov/Learn/PrivacyAct.aspx

US citizens and aliens lawfully admitted for permanent residence may make a request for personal information under the *Privacy Act*. You can file a request by either completing a form or writing a letter to the institution in question, asking for information about yourself, or another individual, as long as that person consents. For instance, if you were making a privacy request to the US Department of Justice (www. justice.gov/usao/resources/making-foia-request/foia-frequently-asked-questions#4) you would write a letter, or complete a form (www.justice. gov/sites/default/files/oip/legacy/2014/07/23/cert_ind.pdf). Be sure to provide enough detail to allow staff to identify the relevant records.

If seeking information about yourself, you'll be required to verify your identity in order to ensure the records are not disclosed to someone else.

There is no fee. Agencies have 20 working days to respond, though that length of time can vary depending on circumstances such as workload and the complexity of the request. Upon receipt of the request, the department will send an acknowledgment letter with a tracking number.

The outcome of a *Privacy Act* request may be appealed.

2. Accessing Your Information in Canada

Canada's privacy framework consists of a network of laws operating at multiple legal layers, backed up by active privacy commissioners and a judiciary that is alive to the importance of protecting privacy in the digital age. Although navigating them can sometimes be complex, taken as a whole, Canada's privacy laws provide some of the most effective and comprehensive privacy protections in the world.

At the federal level, there are two privacy laws that protect your information: The first is the *Privacy Act*, which covers about 250 departments, agencies, and Crown corporations, ranging from Indigenous Affairs and Northern Development Canada to the Yukon Surface Rights Board. The second is the *Personal Information Protection and Electronic Documents Act*, which covers many private-sector organizations.

The *Privacy Act* —

- sets rules for how the federal government collects, retains, uses, and discloses your personal information;

- gives you the legal right to access and correct information held about you by the federal government; and

- puts in place and empowers an ombudsman, the Privacy Commissioner.

Canadian citizens, permanent residents, and individuals present in Canada may make a *Privacy Act* request.

You can file an application with a federal organization by completing a Personal Information Request Form (see Sample 6) or writing a letter. As in the US, there is no fee. If you are writing a letter, be clear that you're requesting information under the *Privacy Act*. Some agencies now accept requests electronically.

Send the request to the Access to Information and Privacy coordinator of the agency you believe holds your information (www.tbs-sct. gc.ca/hgw-cgf/oversight-surveillance/atip-aiprp/coord-eng.asp).

It's important to identify yourself so the agency can be sure it is actually you asking for your personal information. The institution might contact you to verify your identity and to confirm that you have a right of access. You should also outline the information you are seeking, as being precise can speed things along.[2] Under the law, the institution in question has 30 calendar days to respond, though it may take a 30-day extension.

To find out more about the process and how it works, visit the Office of the Privacy Commissioner's website (priv.gc.ca).

2   Frequently Asked Questions: How Do I Make a Request for My Personal Information, Office of the Privacy Commissioner of Canada, accessed March 2016. priv.gc.ca/faqs/index_e.asp#q008

PERSONAL INFORMATION REQUEST FORM

Info Source

Personal Information Request Form

Protected when completed

For official use only

Note: Please refer to page 2 for further information.

Federal government institution

I wish to examine the information

☐ as it is   ☐ in English   ☐ in French

Provide details regarding the personal information being sought (e.g. subject matter, date range, type of records)

Method of access preferred
(Please choose one)

☐ Receive paper copies of the documents
☐ Receive electronic copies of the documents
☐ Examine the documents in government offices

Name of applicant

Street, address, apartment   City or town

Province   Postal Code   Telephone number

☐ I am a Canadian citizen, permanent resident, or an individual present in Canada, and request personal information about myself.

☐ I request personal information on behalf of another individual who is a Canadian citizen, permanent resident or an individual present in Canada.

Date

Please note that the institution may contact you to verify your identity and to confirm that you have a right of access under the *Privacy Act*.

The personal information provided on this form is protected under the provisions of the *Access to Information Act* and the *Privacy Act* and is retained and used as described in Personal Information Bank PSU 901 of the institution to which this form is submitted.

TBC/CTC 350-0058E (Rev. 06/2014)

Canadä

Source: Treasury Board Secretariat of Canada
(tbs-sct.gc.ca/tbsf-fsct/350-58-nfeng.pdf)

If you are unhappy with the length of time it's taking to deal with your request, or the amount of material the institution ultimately discloses, you can complain. The process is described in more detail on the Privacy Commissioner's website (priv.gc.ca/complaint-plainte/index_e.asp).

The *Personal Information Protection and Electronic Documents Act* (PIPEDA) is the rulebook for how private-sector organizations collect, use, and disclose personal information. It also covers the personal information of employees of federally regulated organizations such as airlines, banks, and telecommunications firms. PIPEDA generally does not apply to charities and other nonprofit organizations. In addition, there are exceptions when a province has legislation considered "substantially similar" to PIPEDA.[3]

In seeking access to your information under PIPEDA, you may submit a written request to the organization believed to have your personal information. You must provide sufficient detail — such as account numbers or the names of people you may have dealt with — to help the agency identify the records you want. Organizations must give you the information sought within a reasonable time and at little or no cost.

Under both the *Privacy Act* and PIPEDA you may complain to the Privacy Commissioner if you feel your personal information has been inappropriately handled. The commissioner is also responsible for enforcing elements of Canada's anti-spam law.

Here is the complaint form (plainte-complaint.priv.gc.ca/en) as well as more on the process (priv.gc.ca/complaint-plainte/index_e.asp).

Confused about where to turn with your privacy issue in Canada? The Privacy Commissioner has prepared a handy guide to help (priv.gc.ca/information/pub/guide_ind_e.asp).

---

3   Privacy Legislation in Canada, Office of the Privacy Commissioner of Canada, accessed March 2016. priv.gc.ca/resource/fs-fi/02_05_d_15_e.asp

9
The Future

The unstoppable march of technology will continue to spawn new privacy challenges. Innovations once so complex or expensive that they were limited to the laboratory or university setting have become readily accessible and commercialized. Many of these advances present risks for what might be the final frontier of privacy, the human body.

I. Genetic Testing

It still seems like the stuff of science fiction, but for about $200 you can explore your own DNA through genetic testing.

One company, 23andMe — named for the 23 pairs of chromosomes in the nucleus of most cells — provides you with reports on more than 100 health conditions and traits, data about inherited risk factors, and how you might respond to certain medications, as well as information on your ancestral lineage.

While the company promises to tell you about traits such as male pattern baldness and lactose intolerance, it acknowledges life insurance companies or employers might ask for your genetic information, or whether you have had a test.

The Canadian Life and Health Insurance Association code for member companies says while insurers will not ask that tests be done, they may request that existing genetic test results be made available to the insurer for the purposes of classifying risk. The association maintains that an insurance contract is a "good faith" agreement and that both the

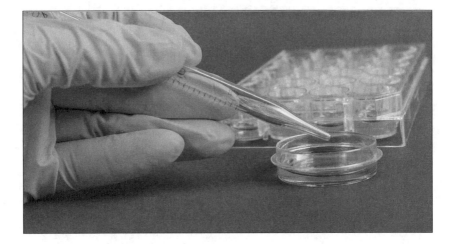

applicant and insurer have an obligation to disclose any information that may be relevant.[1]

The federal privacy commissioner has urged the industry association to go further and refrain from requesting access to existing genetic test results "until such time as they can be shown to be demonstrably necessary and effective."[2] For the vast majority of genetic tests, the ability to predict health and life outcomes with any reasonable degree of certainty was still relatively low, the watchdog said.

The commissioner has supported proposed legislation to prohibit any person from requiring an individual to undergo a genetic test or disclose the results of a genetic test as a condition of providing goods or services to, or entering into a contract with, the individual. As of mid-2016, the latest version of the bill was making its way through Parliament.

In the United States, the *Genetic Information Nondiscrimination Act* of 2008 prohibits a health insurer from requiring a genetic test or denying benefits as a result of a pre-existing condition stemming from a genetic test result.

1   "Industry Code: Genetic Testing Information for Insurance Underwriting," Canadian Life and Health Insurance Association, accessed March 2016. clhia.ca/domino/html/clhia/CLHIA_ LP4W_LND_Webstation.nsf/page/E79687482615DFA485257D5D00682400/$file/Industry_ Code_Genetic_Testing.pdf
2   "Appearance before the Senate Standing Committee on Human Rights on Bill S-201, *An Act to Prohibit and Prevent Genetic Discrimination, The Genetic Non-Discrimination Act*," Office of the Privacy Commissioner of Canada, accessed March 2016. priv.gc.ca/parl/2014/ parl_20141002_e.asp

2. Wearable Devices

You can now wear a wide range of small and smart-looking electronic gizmos that track your mood, movements, and health status as well as details about your immediate environment, including location, images, sounds, temperature, and humidity. For instance, the popular Fitbit can monitor steps taken and calories burned during the day and measure how well you sleep at night — data that can be viewed and analyzed through a smartphone app.

As more and more information about our bodies is collected and digitized through wearable computing devices and connected with other online and offline information about us, the impacts can be profound, Canadian Privacy Commissioner Daniel Therrien's office said in a report on key priorities.

"The integration of technology in the human body is certainly something to watch for in the future," Therrien said in a recent interview with The Canadian Press. "It's a growing phenomenon, obviously, and it's something we'll be trying to monitor as best we can."

3. Big Data

Number crunching has clearly caught the eye of senior decision-makers. The following examples were highlighted in a May 2015 presentation, Big Data Analytics in the World of Safety and Security, for Public Safety Canada's internal policy committee:[3]

- The Philadelphia police mined data to predict a parolee's risk of reoffending to determine the necessary level of supervision.

- US researchers found that a genetic variant related to schizophrenia was not detectable when reviewing 3,500 cases but were able to pinpoint a trend by looking at 35,000 cases.

- In Guatemala, a pilot project revealed how mobile phone movement patterns could be used to predict socioeconomic status.

Big data analytics generally refers to the process of gathering and systematically sifting through millions or even billions of pieces of data (e.g., numbers, text, graphics, videos, sensor information) to glean insights that can't be detected through standard methods.

In the United States, the White House has championed big data as an opportunity to boost economic productivity, drive improved consumer and government services, thwart terrorism, and save lives — all while protecting American core values.

Years ago, Jennifer Stoddart, Canadian privacy commissioner at the time, cautioned that big data had not simply increased the risk to privacy — it had changed the very nature of that risk.

The assumption behind big data analytics is that personal data has to be captured — regardless of privacy interests — in the hope that it might be useful at some future point, said Colin Bennett, Political Science Professor at the University of Victoria. This logic flies in the face of a premise of Canadian and international privacy protection law, that organizations should only be capturing personal data for precise, specified, and transparent purposes, Bennett added.

The expanded capacity for data mining, especially the ability to cross-reference various types of personal information, is perhaps the major privacy issue right now, said Vincent Gogolek, Executive Director of the British Columbia Freedom of Information and Privacy Association.

---

3   "Federal Security Officials Eye 'Big Data Analytics' in a Bid to Pinpoint Threats," Jim Bronskill, National Newswatch, accessed March 2016. nationalnewswatch.com/2015/11/12/federal-security-officials-eye-big-data-analytics-in-a-bid-to-pinpoint-threats/#.Vt5K0EB_SSr

"Big data combined with the use of algorithms can result in the creation of what is called a digital persona. However, this digital persona is not an actual person, but a digital shadow which cannot replicate the complete human being," Gogolek said. "How the digital persona is created and what information is used is a highly guarded, proprietary secret, and decisions are increasingly made by machines and systems analyzing this digital shadow. These decisions can involve such important issues as our creditworthiness, eligibility of government programs, or security status — and these decisions can be difficult if not impossible to reverse. The consequences can be catastrophic for the individuals involved."

Gus Hosein, Executive Director of Privacy International in London, wonders whether this will prompt people to try to game the system, and in the process undermine social bonds.

"We will choose our friends online so that our credit profile is improved," Hosein said. "We will only say publicly and read things that are acceptable to others. The repression of our emotions and our ambitions will disturb the human psyche even as we delude ourselves that somehow we are winning."

Privacy does not need to be a barrier to innovative data analytics, the Public Safety presentation says. "We need to think strategically about what we want to accomplish with data and then design in appropriate privacy protections."

Glossary

Adware: Software that displays advertisements on your computer. Adware becomes a problem if it installs itself on your computer without your consent; installs itself in applications other than the one it came with; hijacks your web browser in order to display more ads, or gathers data on your web browsing without your consent and sends it to others. It is designed to be difficult to uninstall.

Antivirus: Software that attempts to protect a device from being taken over by malicious software (or malware). Viruses were some of the first and most prevalent forms of malware; they got their names from the way they would spread from device to device. These days most antivirus software is designed to warn against downloading a suspicious file from an external source, and will examine files on your computer to see if they match the software's idea of what malware looks like.

App: An app is a type of software that allows you to perform specific tasks. Applications for desktop or laptop computers are sometimes called "desktop applications," and those for mobile devices are called "mobile apps." When you open an application, it runs inside the operating system until you close it.

Asset: In threat modeling, any piece of data or device that needs to be protected. For example, your email, contact lists, instant messages, and files are all assets. Your devices are also assets.

Big data analytics: The strategy of analyzing large volumes of data, or big data. This big data is gathered from a wide variety of sources, including social networks, videos, digital images, sensors, and sales transaction records. The aim in analyzing all this data is to uncover patterns and connections that might otherwise be invisible, and that might provide valuable insights about the users who created it.

Compromise: The unauthorized access to, or disclosure, destruction, removal, modification, use, or interruption of assets or information.

Cookies: A technology that allows websites to recognize your browser. Cookies were originally designed to allow sites to offer online shopping carts, save preferences, or keep you logged on to a site. They also enable tracking and profiling so sites can recognize you and learn more about where you go, which devices you use, and what you are interested in — even if you don't have an account with that site, or aren't logged on to it.

Denial of Service Attack (DoS Attack) or Distributed Denial of Service Attack (DDoS): A type of cyberattack aimed at overwhelming or otherwise disrupting the ability of the target system to receive information and interact with any other system (e.g., sending unwanted messages to keep a server or network from working).

Digital literacy: Describes the range of skills needed by individuals to make wise, informed and ethical online decisions. Privacy management is one of the core skills necessary for digital literacy. Digital literacy is considered a central component of a larger digital economy strategy.

Disclosure: Refers to the release of personal information by any method (e.g., transmission, provision of a copy, examination of a record) to any person.

Do not track: A mechanism for protecting online privacy that specifically addresses the challenge of pervasive online web tracking, especially as employed by behavioral advertisers using increasingly sophisticated tracking technologies. Do not track combines both technology (a signal transmitted from a user) as well as a policy framework for how companies that receive the signal should respond.

Encryption: A process that takes a message and makes it unreadable except to a person who knows how to decrypt it back into a readable form.

Every reasonable effort: Means a level of effort that a fair and reasonable person would expect or would find acceptable.

Flash Cookies: Flash cookies (also called Local Shared Objects or LSOs) are created by Adobe's popular Flash browser add-on for multimedia. Similar to traditional cookies, Flash cookies can be used to save information, as well as preferences, between sessions. They are also used to track the websites that you visit. These cookies are normally not visible to you and options to control or delete them are usually absent or very difficult to find. Flash cookies are frequently found on websites, and they are often used along with traditional web cookies.

HTTPS (Hypertext Transfer Protocol): If you've ever seen a web address spelled out as http://www.example.com/, you'll recognize the http bit of this term. HTTP is the way a web browser on your machine talks to a remote web server. Unfortunately, standard http sends text insecurely across the Internet. HTTPS (the S stands for "secure") uses encryption to better protect the data you send to websites, and the information they return to you, from prying eyes.

HTTPS Everywhere: HTTPS Everywhere is a Firefox, Chrome, and Opera extension that encrypts your communications with many major websites, making your browsing more secure.

Identity theft: The preparatory stage of acquiring and collecting someone else's personal information for criminal purposes.

Identity Theft Report: A police report that contains information specific enough for a creditor to determine the legitimacy of the identity theft claims. This usually is more detailed than a typical police report and best procured by filing a local police report and attaching or incorporating the information from the Identity Theft Affidavit.

Internet of Things (IoT): An environment in which objects, animals, or people are provided with unique identifiers and the ability to transfer data over a network without requiring human-to-human or human-to-computer interaction. IoT has evolved from the convergence of wireless technologies, micro-electromechanical systems (MEMS), and the Internet. The concept may also be referred to as the Internet of Everything.

A thing can be a person with a heart monitor implant, a farm animal with a biochip transponder, an automobile that has built-in sensors to alert the driver when tire pressure is low — or any other natural or man-made object that can be assigned an IP address and provided with the ability to transfer data over a network.

IP Address: A device on the Internet needs its own address to receive data, just like a home or business needs a street address to receive physical mail. This address is its IP (Internet Protocol) address. When you connect to a website or other server online, you usually reveal your own IP address. This doesn't necessarily reveal your identity (it's hard to map an IP address to a real address or a particular computer). An IP address can give away some information about you (e.g., rough location or the name of your Internet Service Provider). Services like Tor let you hide your IP address, which helps give you anonymity online.

Malicious software: Malware is short for malicious software — programs that are designed to conduct unwanted actions on your device. Computer viruses are malware. So are programs that steal passwords, secretly record you, or delete your data.

Man-in-the-middle attack: Suppose you believe you were speaking to your friend, Bahram, via encrypted instant messenger. To check it's really him, you ask him to tell you the city where you first met. "Istanbul" comes the reply. That's correct! Unfortunately, without you or Bahram knowing, someone else online has been intercepting all your communications. When you first connected to Bahram, you actually connected to this person, and she, in turn, connected to Bahram. When you think you are asking Bahram a question, she receives your message, relays the question to Bahram, receives his answer back, and then sends it to you. Even though you think you are communicating securely with Bahram, you are, in fact, only communicating securely with the spy, who is also communicating securely to Bahram! This is the man-in-the-middle attack. These middlemen can spy on communications or even insert false or misleading messages into your communications.

Material privacy breach: A breach that involves sensitive personal information and could reasonably be expected to cause injury or harm to the individual and/or involves a large number of affected individuals.

Metadata: Metadata (or data about data) is everything about a piece of information, apart from the information itself. So the content of a message is not metadata, but who sent it, when, from where, and to whom, are all examples of metadata. Legal systems often protect content to a greater degree than they protect metadata (e.g., in the US, law enforcement needs a warrant to listen to a person's telephone calls, but claims the right to obtain the list of who you have called far more easily). Metadata can often reveal a great deal, and will often need to be protected as carefully as the data it describes.

Password safe: Allows you to use different difficult-to-guess passwords for all your services, without needing to remember them. Instead, you only need to remember one master password that allows you to decrypt a database of all your passwords. Password safes are convenient and allow you to organize all of your passwords in one location.

Perma-cookie: It stays on your hard drive and can be read by any web server that you visit and be used to build a profile of your Internet habits.

Personal information: Information about an identifiable individual that is recorded in any form. This includes name, address, telephone number, medical/clinical information, identification numbers, education, blood type, ethnicity, and employee files.

Personal information bank: A description of personal information that is organized and retrievable by a person's name or by an identifying number, symbol, or other particular assigned only to that person. The personal data described in the bank is available for an administrative purpose of a government institution.

Phishing: An attempt to obtain personal information for identity theft, or other sensitive information such as credit card numbers or bank account details for fraud. For example, an email message may appear to be from the recipient's bank asking him or her to visit a website to confirm account details, but instead directs the person to a false website where the personal information is collected. A variation of phishing called "spear-phishing" gains and uses specific information about users to tailor these fake emails so they seem even more real.

Privacy: The right of an individual to be left alone, to be free of unwarranted intrusions. It is also the right of an individual to retain control over his or her personal information and to know the use, disclosure, and whereabouts of that information.

Privacy breach: Involves improper or unauthorized creation, collection, use, disclosure, retention, or disposal of personal information.

Privacy impact assessment: A policy process for identifying, assessing, and mitigating privacy risks. Government institutions are to develop and maintain privacy impact assessments for all new or modified programs and activities that involve the use of personal information for an administrative purpose.

Privacy practices: Refers to all practices related to the creation, collection, retention, accuracy, use, disclosure, and disposition of personal information.

Risk: Denotes the effect of uncertainty on objectives. It is the expression of the likelihood and impact of an event with the potential to affect the achievement of an organization's objectives.

Revenge porn: The online distribution of sexual images without the consent of the subject.

Right to be forgotten: Individuals have the right, under certain conditions, to ask search engines to remove links with personal information about them. This applies where the information is inaccurate, inadequate, irrelevant, or excessive for the purposes of the data processing. However, the right to be forgotten is not absolute, but will always need to be balanced against other fundamental rights, such as the freedom of expression and publication through the media. The role of the person requesting the deletion might also be relevant. That is, the right to be forgotten is certainly not about making prominent people less prominent or making criminals less criminal.

Risk management: A systematic approach to setting the best course of action under uncertainty by identifying, assessing, understanding, making decisions on, and communicating risk issues. Risk management is built into existing governance and organizational structures, such as business planning, decision-making, and operational processes.

Smart TV: As an adjective the word "smart" is used to describe a new device capable of more advanced functions. A Smart TV is created by adding computing power to a television, allowing you to play video games, conduct Internet searches, and connect to other devices such as laptops and phones. A Smart TV comes with its own operating system.

Spam: Generally refers to the use of electronic messaging systems to send unsolicited, bulk messages. Spam messages may contain deceptive content, support illegal activities, and be used to deliver electronic threats such as spyware and viruses.

Spoofing: Pretending to be another person or organization to make it appear that an email message originated from somewhere other than its actual source.

Spyware: Software that collects information about a user without the user's knowledge or consent. Some spyware changes the way a user's computer works.

Third-party cookies: Initially, cookies were only shared between the website (the "first party" in the transaction) and the user (the "second party"). Soon after cookies were invented their use was expanded to third parties — organizations not directly involved in the interaction — such as advertising companies displaying ads on certain websites. When an advertisement is on a web page supplied by a first party, the advertising content and a cookie are passed from the advertising company (the third party) to the end user's (your) computer. When you revisit that same first-party website, or another site that uses the same advertising company, the third-party cookie can be retrieved by the advertising company. If the cookie contains a unique identifier, then information about your visits to different websites can be linked together. (Also see cookies.)

Trojan virus: A type of malware that can infect a computer and spreads by copying itself and using the infected computer to send itself to other computers. Viruses are generally spread by email or website pop-ups.

Two-factor authentication: Login systems that require only a username and password risk being broken when someone else can obtain (or guess) those pieces of information. Services that offer two-factor authentication require you to provide a separate confirmation that you are who you say you are. The second factor could be a one-off secret code, a number generated by a program running on a mobile device, or a device that you carry and that you can use to confirm who you are. Companies such as banks and major Internet services (e.g., Google, PayPal, Twitter) now offer two-factor authentication.

Vehicle telematics: The application of both telecommunications and informatics to deliver value-added services (e.g., voice navigation systems) for use in vehicles.

VPN (virtual private network): A method of connecting your computer securely to the network of an organization on the other side of the Internet. When you use a VPN, all of your computer's Internet communications are packaged together, encrypted, and then relayed to this other organization, where it is decrypted, unpacked, and then sent on to its destination. To the organization's network, or any other computer on the wider Internet, it looks like your computer's request is coming from inside the organization, not from your location.

Web browser: The program you use to view websites (e.g., Firefox, Safari, Internet Explorer, Chrome). Smartphones have a built-in web-browser app for the same purpose.

Zombie: A computer infected by malware that is remotely controlled by the maker, distributor, or controller of the malware. Most spam is currently sent through zombies.

Resources

I. Privacy

"The Internet of Things Research Study"
Hewlett Packard
    www8.hp.com/h20195/V2/GetPDF.aspx/4AA5-4759ENW.pdf

Privacy Handbook
BC Civil Liberties Association
    bccla.org/privacy-handbook/privacy5contents.html

United States Department of Justice
(Office of Privacy and Civil Liberties)
Frequently Asked Questions
    justice.gov/opcl/faq

Office of the Privacy Commissioner of Canada
"Ten Tips for Protecting Personal Information"
    priv.gc.ca/resource/fs-fi/02_05_d_64_tips_e.asp

"Ten Tips for Reducing the Likelihood of a Privacy Breach"
    priv.gc.ca/resource/fs-fi/02_05_d_60_tips_e.asp

A Guide for Individuals: Protecting Your Privacy
    priv.gc.ca/information/pub/guide_ind_e.asp

Electronic Frontier Foundation
Surveillance Self-Defense
Eva Galperin, Global Policy Analyst
    ssd.eff.org/en

2. Fraud

Canadian Anti-Fraud Centre
  antifraudcentre-centreantifraude.ca/reportincident-signalerincident/
  index-eng.htm

Canadian Spam Reporting Centre
  fightspam.gc.ca/eic/site/030.nsf/eng/h_00017.html

Federal Trade Commission
  identitytheft.gov

Guide for Assisting Identity Theft Victims
  consumer.ftc.gov/articles/pdf-0119-guide-assisting-id-theft-
  victims.pdf

United States Department of Justice
Report Fraud
  justice.gov/criminal-fraud/report-fraud

3. Blocking Cookies and Creating Passwords

For blocking cookies:

- Ghostery.com

- AdblockPlus.org

Password management tool:

- truekey.com

"Alternatives to Passwords: Replacing the Ubiquitous Authenticator"
Ron Condon, ComputerWeekly.com
  computerweekly.com/feature/Alternatives-to-passwords-Replacing-
  the-ubiquitous-authenticator

The Diceware Passphrase

To help you create a strong, but easy to remember passphrase:

- world.std.com/~reinhold/diceware.html

- world.std.com/~reinhold/diceware.wordlist.asc

Animated guide to Diceware:

- ssd.eff.org/en/module/animated-overview-how-make-super-secure-password-using-dice

4. Transparency

Public Safety Canada, Annual Report on the Use of Electronic Surveillance
Government of Canada
> publications.gc.ca/site/eng/360588/publication.html

Transparency Reporting by Private Sector Companies
Office of the Privacy Commissioner of Canada
> priv.gc.ca/information/research-recherche/2015/transp_201506_e.asp

Transparency Reporting Guidelines
Innovation, Science and Economic Development Canada
> ic.gc.ca/eic/site/smt-gst.nsF/eng/sf11057.html

Wiretap Reports
United States Courts
> uscourts.gov/statistics-reports/analysis-reports/wiretap-reports

"Who Has Your Back? Protecting Your Data from Government Requests"
Electronic Frontier Foundation
> eff.org/who-has-your-back-government-data-requests-2015

"What Transparency Reports Don't Tell Us"
Ryan Budish, *The Atlantic*
> theatlantic.com/technology/archive/2013/12/what-transparency-reports-dont-tell-us/282529

"I Downloaded My Facebook Data. Here's What I Got"
Craig Desson, The Toronto Star
> thestar.com/news/privacy-blog/2015/09/i-downloaded-my-facebook-data-here-s-what-i-got.html

Europe versus Facebook
Austrian privacy watchdog Max Schrems
> europe-v-facebook.org/EN/Get_your_Data_/get_your_data_.html

5. Encryption, App Security, and Smartphones

Encryption
  advocacy.mozilla.org/encrypt

Get Smart on the Web
(Especially Government Surveillance: Try encryption)
  mozilla.org/en-US/teach/smarton/surveillance/?utm_
  source=desktop-snippet&utm_medium=snippet&utm_
  content=smarton&utm_term=5440&utm_campaign=
  smarton&sample_rate=0.1&snippet_name=5440

Security in-a-Box
(For activists and human rights defenders)
  securityinabox.org

"Exposing Your Personal Information -- There's an App for That"
Daniel V. Hoffman, Juniper Networks
  forums.juniper.net/t5/Security-Now/Exposing-Your-Personal-
  Information-There-s-An-App-for-That/ba-p/166058

"Regulatory Guidance: Mobile Privacy, Tracking & Advertising"
Samuelson-Glushko Canadian Internet Policy and Public Interest Clinic
(CIPPIC)
  cippic.ca/index.php?q=en/mobile_privacy_guidelines

Ten Tips for Individuals on Protecting Personal Information on Mobile
Devices (OPC)
  priv.gc.ca/resource/fs-fi/02_05_d_47_dpd_e.asp

"What Sean Penn Teaches Us About How Not to Chat With a Fugitive"
Andrew Fishman, *The Intercept*
  theintercept.com/2016/01/12/sean-penn-el-chapo-opsec

"How to be invisible: Designers Create Anti-Surveillance Products to
Protect Privacy"
Laura Beeston, *The Globe and Mail*
  theglobeandmail.com/life/anti-surveillance-items-helping-people-
  go-off-the-grid/article26805195

"Ways to be Secret"
Victoria and Albert Museum
  vam.ac.uk/designandpubliclife/2015/06/15/ways-to-be-secret

6. Border Security

"Defending Privacy at the US Border: A Guide for Travelers Carrying Digital Devices"
Seth Schoen, Marcia Hofmann, and Rowan Reynolds, Electronic Frontier Foundation
    eff.org/files/eff-border-search_2.pdf

US Customs and Border Protection
Submit a Complaint/Concern
    help.cbp.gov/app/forms/complaint

Watch Lists & Border Controls
    travelwatchlist.ca

Terrorist Screening Center (US)
    fbi.gov/about-us/nsb/tsc/terrorist-screening-center-frequently-asked-questions

"How the US's Terrorism Watchlists Work -- and How You Could End up on One"
Spencer Ackerman, *The Guardian*
    theguardian.com/world/2014/jul/24/us-terrorism-watchlist-work-no-fly-list

Transportation Security Administration
Complaints
    tsa.gov/contact-center/form/complaints

Security screening
    tsa.gov/travel/security-screening

US Department of Homeland Security
File a *Privacy Act* Request
    dhs.gov/file-privacy-act-request

Freedom of Information Act and Privacy Act
    dhs.gov/freedom-information-act-and-privacy-act

Office for Civil Rights and Civil Liberties
    dhs.gov/office-civil-rights-and-civil-liberties

Traveler Redress Inquiry Program
    tsa.gov/travel/passenger-support/travel-redress-program

Canadian Air Transport Security Authority (CATSA)
1-888-294-2202

Complaints
catsa.gc.ca/questions-comments-and-complaints

Damaged or lost items
catsa.gc.ca/claims

Security Screening
catsa.gc.ca/breezethrough

Public Safety Canada
Application to the Passenger Protect Recourse Office Form under the Passenger Protect Program
publicsafety.gc.ca/cnt/ntnl-scrt/cntr-trrrsm/pssngr-prtct/pplctn-frm-eng.aspx

Safeguarding Canadians with Passenger Protect
publicsafety.gc.ca/cnt/ntnl-scrt/cntr-trrrsm/pssngr-prtct/index-en.aspx

7. Key Intelligence Watchdogs

Canadian Security Intelligence Review Committee
www.sirc.gc.ca/cmpplt/mkeprt-eng.html

Office of the Communications Security Establishment Commissioner
ocsec-bccst.gc.ca/s58/d313/eng/complaints-procedure

Civilian Review and Complaints Commission for the RCMP
crcc-ccetp.gc.ca

US Department of Justice
Office of the Inspector General
oig.justice.gov

National Security Agency (NSA)
Office of the Inspector General
www.nsa.gov/about/oig/

Central Intelligence Agency (CIA)
Inspector General
cia.gov/offices-of-cia/inspector-general